GW01458863

Sissy School: A Comprehensive Guide to Feminization Training

Mistress LaLa

Published by Mistress LaLa, 2024.

SISSY SCHOOL: A COMPREHENSIVE GUIDE TO FEMINIZATION TRAINING

First edition. May 17, 2024.

Copyright © 2024 Mistress LaLa.

ISBN: 979-8223577034

Written by Mistress LaLa.

Table of Contents

Preface

Welcome, dear reader, to a journey of transformation and self-discovery. "Sissy School: A Comprehensive Guide to Feminization Training" is designed to guide those who wish to explore the sissy persona, a term used widely in the context of gender expression and feminization. Whether you are taking your first tentative steps into this world, or you are looking to deepen your existing understanding and practice, this book promises a comprehensive path toward embracing a feminine persona through carefully curated assignments and supportive insights.

The culture of feminization training involves adopting traditionally feminine traits, behaviors, and roles, and this book adopts a consensual, respectful, and constructive approach to such transformations. Our aim is not only to provide you with practical steps but also to foster a safe space for personal growth and exploration of your identity in a nuanced, celebratory way.

The assignments within these pages cover a wide range of topics—from wardrobe and makeup tips to voice modulation and behavioral adjustments. Each task has been thoughtfully designed to progressively guide you through your transformation journey in an empathetic, structured, and enjoyable manner. The exercises are scalable and can be adjusted to suit your pace and comfort level, making this guide suitable for both novices and those more experienced in the art of feminization.

As you work through "Sissy School", you will find more than just assignments. The book is peppered with stories, advice, and motivational guidance to help you navigate any challenges that might arise, ensuring a holistic approach to learning and transformation. We touch upon the psychological aspects of feminization and gender identity, empowering you to find balance and harmony within your evolving sissy persona.

Embarking on this journey requires openness, bravery, and, most importantly, a commitment to self-love and acceptance. Remember, this transformation, much like any meaningful journey in life, is deeply personal and subjective. It is imperative to approach each step with a sense of curiosity and respect for oneself and the diverse expressions of gender.

"Sissy School" is your playbook and companion in the fascinating world of feminization. May you find joy, enlightenment, and perhaps a new side of yourself within its pages. Let us begin this captivating adventure together.

With warmth and encouragement,

Mistress LaLa

Author and Guide from **myprettysissy.com**

Chapter 1: Introduction to Sissy Feminization

What is Sissy Feminization?

Welcome to the first step on your fabulous journey into sissy feminization! If you're curious about what it means to embrace the sissy persona, you've come to the right place. Sissy feminization is a dynamic and transformative process, where individuals (usually assigned male at birth) explore and adopt traditionally feminine traits, roles, and aesthetics. It's not just about outward appearances; it's about redefining one's identity and experiences through a feminine lens.

Understanding the Basics

At its heart, sissy feminization is about self-expression and transformation. It involves various aspects like cross-dressing, behaving, and engaging in activities traditionally associated with women. This practice aims to explore gender identity, often as a form of personal fulfillment or erotic pleasure. For some, it's a deeply private part of their lifestyle, while for others, it might be shared with a community of like-minded individuals.

More Than Just Dressing Up

While putting on a dress and makeup might be the most visible elements, becoming a sissy involves much more. It encompasses learning about feminine posture, movements, and etiquette. It's about adopting a persona that aligns with your innermost desires and presenting yourself in a way that feels right.

Exploring the Why and How

People are drawn to sissy feminization for various reasons. Some find empowerment in the vulnerability and submission associated with traditional femininity. Others might find joy in breaking societal norms and expressing a part of themselves that they've kept hidden. No matter the reason, it's a deeply personal journey that is as unique as the individuals who embark on it.

A Path to Self-Discovery

Sissy feminization can be a path to understanding more about one's identity, preferences, and desires. It often involves a significant amount of introspection and can be a powerful mode of self-expression and acceptance. Whether you're looking for ways to spice up your personal life or simply exploring aspects of your gender identity, feminization can be a rewarding experience.

Join the Community

You're not alone in this journey! There's a vibrant, supportive community out there with experienced sissies who have been where you are now. Engaging with community forums, attending events, or even connecting with others online can provide valuable support, advice, and camaraderie as you explore the nuances of feminization.

As you turn the pages of this guide, remember that every step you take is personal and customizable. There's no right or wrong way to be a sissy—what matters most is your comfort and happiness. Embrace the journey, enjoy your transformation, and let your inner sissy princess shine!

. . ᦔᦱ . .

History and Culture of Sissy Training

HELLO AND WELCOME, future sissy princesses! If you're starting your journey into the fascinating world of sissy training, understanding its rich history and culture is key to embracing your new path. Let's dive into the delightful and intricate world of sissy feminization that has evolved throughout the years into the phenomenon it is today!

The Roots of Sissy Training

Sissy training, although it might seem modern, has historical roots that stretch back further than you might imagine. The term "sissy" itself originates from the word "sister" and was traditionally used as a pejorative for men deemed too effeminate or lacking masculinity according to societal standards. Over time, however, the sissy community has reclaimed the word, transforming it into a label worn with pride and joy.

The practice of feminization – dressing and behaving in a traditionally feminine manner – can be traced back to theatrical traditions and courtly masquerades, where men often donned women's clothing and played feminine roles. This was not only an artistic expression but also a subtle subversion of gender norms. In more modern times, this transformational experience became a part of the broader spectrum of BDSM and fetish subcultures, making it more structured and defined.

The Cultural Significance

In the contemporary context, sissy training is more than just cross-dressing or playing a temporary role. It is a deep, personal journey that involves both psychological and physical transformation. The culture of sissy training embraces themes of submission, sexuality, and identity exploration, often within the safe confines of a supportive community that values consent and personal boundaries.

Expansion Through Modern Media

With the advent of the internet, the visibility of the sissy training culture has grown exponentially. Online forums, blogs, and websites dedicated to feminization guide those new to the culture through their transformations. These platforms also connect individuals across the globe, creating a nurturing environment where one can share experiences, advice, and encouragement.

Moreover, the portrayal of sissy training in films, literature, and especially online media has played a significant role in normalizing the practice and informing the public about this unique lifestyle choice. It's a vibrant culture rich with diversity, where each individual's journey is celebrated as uniquely beautiful.

Embracing the Journey

As we delve deeper into the world of sissy training throughout this book, remember that this journey is yours to define. Whether for personal discovery, expression of a hidden part of oneself, or just the sheer joy of it, the path of feminization is as rewarding as it is transformative.

Understanding the history and culture of sissy training will not only enrich your personal experience but also connect you to a community with a fascinating past and an exciting future. So, lace up your prettiest heels, adjust your tiara, and prepare to walk boldly (and fabulously) into the world of sissy training!

. . ⚘ . .

Benefits of Embracing Your Sissy Self

WELCOME TO YOUR EXCITING journey into the world of sissy feminization! If you're new here or just curious about the benefits of embracing this unique identity, you're in the right place. Understanding the advantages of stepping into your sissy self can deepen your commitment and enhance your personal experience. Let's explore how adopting this lifestyle can positively transform your life.

Personal Freedom and Self-Expression

One of the most significant benefits of embracing your sissy self is the incredible sense of liberation it brings. In our everyday lives, societal norms often dictate how we express ourselves, especially concerning gender roles. But as a sissy, you can break free from these constraints! It's all about expressing your inner femininity, something that may have been suppressed for too long. This journey is about finding and celebrating your true self without apologies.

Increased Confidence and Acceptance

Many find that stepping into their sissy identity comes with a surprising boost in confidence. Yes, it might sound counterintuitive given the vulnerability of gender expression, but it's about embracing who you are completely. This acceptance of your inner self is empowering. As you learn to walk, talk, and carry yourself in ways that feel innate and joyful, you'll discover a profound appreciation for your uniqueness, boosting your self-esteem and overall confidence.

Community and Friendship

The sissy community is vibrant, supportive, and growing every day. Engaging with others who share your interests and experiences can be incredibly rewarding. As you dive into sissy feminization, you'll find forums, social media groups, and events where you can connect, share tips, and form lasting friendships. This community can be a fantastic source of support, advice, and camaraderie.

Emotional and Psychological Growth

Embracing your sissy self often leads to significant emotional and psychological development. This path encourages introspection and self-discovery. You'll explore aspects of your personality and desires that might have been ignored or unknown. This deep, internal work can be challenging but also immensely rewarding, leading to greater emotional resilience and clarity.

Creativity and Play

Sissy feminization is a playground for creativity! From fashion and makeup to behavior and speech, you get to redesign yourself. This process is not just about aesthetics; it's a full embrace of creativity and experimentation. Each step—from choosing your outfit to perfecting your sissy mannerisms—allows you to engage in a deeply personal and creative act, adding a splash of color and excitement to your life.

Empowerment Through Learning New Skills

As you embark on this journey, you'll acquire a host of new skills. These can range from mastering makeup techniques to understanding the nuances of feminine body language. Each new skill you learn not only enhances your ability to present as a sissy but also contributes to a sense of achievement and empowerment. It's about setting personal goals and celebrating each victory along the way.

In conclusion, embracing your sissy self can open up a world of benefits that touch every aspect of your life from personal freedom to emotional growth and community building. This journey is about more than just appearance—it's a holistic transformation that fosters self-expression, confidence, and joy. Remember, the path of feminization is personal and unique to each individual. Embrace it boldly and lovingly, and watch as it enriches your life in ways you never imagined!

So, why wait? Let's step into this fabulous world together and discover the amazing benefits that await on the other side. Your sissy princess transformation is just a chapter away!

Setting Goals for Your Sissy Journey

EMBARKING ON YOUR SISSY feminization journey is an exciting and transformative experience. It's a personal path that involves exploring your identity, embracing femininity, and discovering a whole new side of yourself. But like any significant journey, having a roadmap can make all the difference between wandering aimlessly and reaching your desired destination with flair. In this section, we'll guide you on how to set effective and meaningful goals to enrich your sissy transformation process.

Understanding Why Goals Matter

Goals are essential because they provide direction, motivate you, and give a sense of accomplishment. They help you focus on what's important, track your progress, and stay committed to your transformation journey. For a sissy aspirant, goals might range from attaining a certain level of confidence in feminine attire to mastering the art of makeup or perfecting your sissy etiquette.

Crafting Your Sissy Goals

1. Be Specific: Vague goals are less likely to be achieved. Instead of saying "I want to become more feminine," opt for "I want to learn how to apply daily makeup flawlessly within the next three months."

2. Measure Progress: Ensure your goals are measurable. For example, "I will master walking in high heels by practicing for 30 minutes daily."

3. Attainable and Realistic: It's vital to set goals that are challenging yet achievable. If you have never worn high heels, don't commit to mastering stilettos right away. Start with something more manageable, like kitten heels.

4. Relevant: Your goals should align with your ultimate vision of becoming a sissy princess. Each goal should be a stepping stone towards deeper feminization.

5. Time-Bound: Setting deadlines creates urgency and prompts action. Give yourself a realistic timeline to accomplish each goal.

Some Goal Ideas to Get You Started

- **Appearance Goals:** Define your feminine aesthetic. Whether it's mastering the vintage pin-up look or finding your perfect sissy maid outfit, decide what you want to explore and set goals around achieving this style.

- **Voice and Movement Goals:** Feminine communication isn't just about what you say, but how you say it. Aim to develop a softer tone of voice or learn the art of feminine gestures and poise.

- **Social Interaction Goals:** As your confidence grows, you might want to start going out in public dressed in your sissy attire. Perhaps start with a supportive community event or a private party.

- **Emotional Goals:** Engage with why you want to embark on this journey. Do you seek acceptance, understanding, empowerment? Define these emotional milestones as part of your journey.

Documenting Your Journey

Keeping a journal or blog about your sissy transformation can be tremendously helpful. Document your progress, setbacks, and how you feel about various experiences. This not only serves as a personal account of your journey but can also be a motivational tool when facing challenges.

Celebrate Every Success

No success is too small to celebrate on your journey to becoming a sissy princess. Completing a makeup tutorial, spending a whole day in femme mode, or simply feeling more at peace with your sissy identity are all victories worth recognizing.

Setting clear, achievable goals is the secret to enhancing your sissy transformation journey. By focusing on specific aspects of feminization, you can ensure that every step taken is a positive stride toward your ultimate goal. Now armed with a clearer path, go forth and step confidently into your sissy training with determination and joy!

Understanding the Sissy Mindset

WELCOME TO THE EXCITING world of sissy feminization! Whether you're a newbie curious about this enticing journey or you've dabbled a bit and want to dive deeper, understanding the sissy mindset is your crucial first step. Here in this guide, we'll walk you through what it means to embrace the sissy persona fully, ensuring your transformation is both enjoyable and fulfilling.

Embrace Your Inner Sissy: The sissy mindset begins with acceptance. Accepting your desires and the joys of feminization is essential. It's about acknowledging that your interest in getting dolled up, acting delicately, and embodying femininity is perfectly okay and something to cherish, not hide.

Cultivate Feminine Qualities: Transformation is as much about behavior and attitude as it is about appearance. Think about the qualities typically associated with femininity, such as empathy, gentleness, and a nurturing demeanor. Reflect on how these can be a part of your day-to-day interactions.

Practice Makes Perfect: The journey to becoming a sissy princess is not just an emotional one, but also a practical one. From walking in high heels to mastering makeup, each step is a move towards a more confident and feminine you. Remember, every expert was once a beginner, so keep practicing!

Safety and Consent Are Key: Exploring any new persona, particularly one as vulnerable and open as that of a sissy, means doing so safely and consensually. Always ensure that the environments you are exploring are safe and that the people around you are supportive and understanding of your expressions.

Connect With Community: You're not alone on this journey. Connecting with a community of like-minded individuals can offer support, advice, and friendship. Whether online or in person, finding a network of people who share similar experiences and goals can be deeply enriching.

By embracing the sissy mindset, you're setting the stage for a transformation that transcends physical appearance, touching on emotional depth, personal growth, and an enriching understanding of your own identity. As you continue reading through this guide, keep this foundation in mind—a strong, well-tended root supports the most beautiful blossoms.

Let's get started on this fabulous journey to discovery and freedom. Welcome, soon-to-be sissy princess, to a world where you can proudly showcase your femininity and live your life with joy and gusto! This is just the beginning, and the path ahead is bright and filled with lace, satins, and a whole lot of sparkle. Onward!

Chapter 2: Feminine Presentation Techniques

Mastering Makeup Basics

Hey there, gorgeous! Ready to dive into the glitzy world of makeup? Whether you're a seasoned pro or a beginner, mastering the art of makeup is a crucial step in your transformation journey. Let's get you started on becoming a sissy princess with some makeup basics that will not only enhance your features but also boost your confidence.

Understand Your Skin Type

Before you start experimenting with makeup, it's vital to understand your skin type. Is it oily, dry, combination, or sensitive? This knowledge will guide you in choosing the right products that will work best for you, ensuring your makeup lasts longer and your skin stays healthy.

Foundation: Your Canvas

Think of your face as a canvas and foundation as the base. Foundation helps even out your skin tone and provides a smooth surface for applying other products. Use a shade that matches your skin tone perfectly. For beginners, BB creams or tinted moisturizers are a great start. They're lighter and easier to work with.

Eyes That Mesmerize

Eyes are the windows to the soul, right? Well, let's make them stunning! Beginning with eyeshadows, opt for neutral shades to start. Learn how to blend properly as it's the key to stellar eye makeup. Eyeliner comes next, and a simple trick is to use small dashes along your lash line and connect them for a smoother line. Don't forget mascara—apply from the base of your lashes and wiggle your way up to get a full, luscious look.

Blushing Beauty

A touch of blush can bring your whole face to life. The trick is to keep it natural. Smile and apply the blush on the apples of your cheeks, blending towards the temples. For a subtler look, go for shades like peach or light pink.

Luscious Lips

Lipstick can change your entire look. Start with a lip liner that matches the natural color of your lips to define and enhance your shape. Then, choose a lipstick color that complements your overall makeup. If you're feeling bold, reds and pinks can be your best friends. For everyday wear, nudes and light corals are perfect.

Setting It All

Lastly, you'll want your beautiful work to last. Use a setting spray to help your makeup stay in place throughout your day or event. It also helps prevent smudging and gives you a fresh, dewy finish.

Makeup is not just about colors and products—it's about expressing who you are. It's okay to make mistakes. Remember, practice makes perfect. Each brush stroke adds to your experience, enhancing your skills. So, have fun experimenting with different looks and finding what makes you feel fabulous!

With this guide to basic makeup techniques, you're well on your way to perfecting your sissy princess aesthetic. Each step is a building block to expressing your femininity with confidence and flair. Practice regularly and don't be afraid to try new things. Makeup is an art, and you are its beautiful canvas!

Hair Styling for Sissies

HELLO GORGEOUS! READY to dive into the fabulous world of hair styling? As every sissy knows, your hair is your crown, and getting it just right can truly elevate your sissy transformation. Whether you have flowing locks or a stylish wig, let's make every strand count towards making you the prettiest princess at the ball!

1. Understanding Hair Basics for Sissies

First things first: the type of hair you'll work with. If you're growing your own, great! If not, wigs are a fantastic option that can offer versatility and glamour at a moment's notice. Understand the texture and length of your hair or wig, as this will determine what styles will work best for you.

2. Everyday Sissy Hairstyles

A simple bob, long curls, or bangs can dramatically alter your appearance. Start with basics:

- The Femme Bob: Sleek, easy to maintain, and always elegant.
- Luscious Curls: They require more care, but girls, they're worth it!
- Playful Ponytails and Pigtails: These are not just cute; they're also a nod to classic femininity.

3. Styling Tools and Products

Invest in quality hair styling tools. A reliable straightener, a volumizing blow dryer, and a range of curling irons should be your basic toolkit. As for products, mousse, hair spray, and heat protectant are must-haves to keep everything in place and looking fabulous.

4. Experimenting with Colors

Don't shy away from color experiments! Soft pastels, striking reds, or even multicolored styles can all express different facets of your sissy personality. Always use safe products designed for your hair type or specifically for wigs to avoid any damage.

5. Maintenance and Care

Maintaining the health of your hair or keeping your wig in tip-top shape is crucial. Regular washing, deep conditioning, and proper storage will keep your chosen locks looking fresh and beautiful.

6. Step-by-Step Tutorials

- The Perfect Curl: Wrap small sections around a medium-sized curling iron, hold for 15 seconds, then gently release.

- Sleek and Straight: Use a heat protectant spray before slowly straightening sections for a polished look.

- Stylish Updos: Start practicing simple styles like chignons or French twists that bring an elegant vibe to any outfit.

7. Inspiration and Continual Learning

Follow hairstyling tutorials, Instagram influencers, or blogs dedicated to feminine styles. Watching and learning from others can give you a plethora of ideas and techniques to master that perfect femme look.

Remember, sissies, hair is a big part of your journey and embracing each step of styling it is not just about beauty, it's about expressing your true self. So play, experiment, and enjoy every moment of your transformation—each curl and every strand is a step towards being the fabulous sissy princess you are meant to be!

Keep these tips in mind, and start your journey of personal transformation today by expressing yourself through the mesmerizing art of hair styling.

The Art of Feminine Dressing

WELCOME TO THE VIBRANT world of feminine dressing, where every fabric, color, and style plays a crucial role in your transformation journey into a delightful sissy princess. This section is your personal style guide, helping you navigate through the delightful maze of women's fashion with flair and finesse.

1. Understand the Basics of Women's Clothing

First things first, let's get acquainted with the basics. Women's clothing comes in a variety of shapes, sizes, and styles, each designed to complement different body types and personal tastes. Begin by exploring basic garments such as dresses, skirts, blouses, and trousers. Familiarize yourself with terms like A-line, empire waist, and peplum, which describe different dress and top styles designed to enhance feminine features.

2. Choose Fabrics that Flatter

The choice of fabric can make a huge difference in how your outfit looks and feels. Soft, flowing fabrics like silk, chiffon, and satin suggest delicacy and femininity, perfect for a sissy princess. These materials gently drape over the body, creating an elegant silhouette that's both flattering and comfortable.

3. Colors and Patterns

Embrace the full spectrum of colors and patterns available in women's clothing. Pastel colors like pink, lavender, and baby blue are universally flattering and exude softness and sweetness, ideal for your sissy persona. Don't shy away from floral or delicate patterns, which can add a touch of grace and sophistication to your outfits.

4. The Importance of Proper Fit

Finding the right fit is essential. Clothes that fit well can dramatically enhance your appearance, making you look more polished and put-together. Pay attention to the fit around key areas such as the chest, waist, and hips. A well-fitted outfit should feel comfortable and allow ease of movement without bunching or stretching awkwardly.

5. Accessorize Wisely

Accessories are the finishing touches that can make an outfit shine. From scarves and belts to jewelry and handbags, choosing the right accessories can elevate your look from ordinary to extraordinary. For instance, a simple pearl necklace can add a touch of elegance to a day dress, while a stylish clutch can complement an evening outfit.

6. Shoes: The Foundation of Every Outfit

No outfit is complete without the perfect pair of shoes. Shoes can change the character of an outfit instantly. For your sissy transformation, consider shoes like ballet flats, kitten heels, or classic pumps in neutral or matching colors to maintain that harmonious, feminine appeal.

7. Makeup and Hairstyling Tips

While not clothing per se, your makeup and hairstyle are integral to your overall presentation. Opt for soft, natural makeup to enhance your features subtly. As for hair, whether you choose wigs or style your own hair, aim for styles that frame your face softly and complement your outfit perfectly.

8. Practicing Your Feminine Poise

Lastly, remember that how you wear your clothes is just as important as what you wear. Practice moving gracefully in your new outfits, paying attention to your posture, walking style, and the way you carry yourself.

Diving into the art of feminine dressing is not just about wearing women's clothes—it's about embracing them with confidence and joy. Each item of clothing is a step toward expressing the unique, fabulous sissy princess that you are. So go ahead, explore, and let your wardrobe be a reflection of your inner beauty.

Choosing the Right Accessories

HELLO, DARLING! AS we dive deeper into our sissy princess transformation, let's tackle one of the most fun and fabulous aspects: accessorizing! Accessories are not just embellishments; they play a critical role in expressing your newfound femininity. Like the cherry on top of a glamorous sundown, the right accessories can illuminate your ensemble and bring your entire look together with a sparkle.

Start with the Basics: Jewelry

Jewelry is the quickest way to add a touch of femininity to any outfit. Start with the basics like a cute pair of earrings—hoops or dangles work wonders for elongating the neck and accentuating your cheekbones. Bracelets and rings are next on the list; they not only beautify your hands but also give you a reason to gesture expressively as you chat. And let's not forget the power of a gorgeous necklace to draw eyes to your décolletage.

Step Up Your Game with a Sissy Princess Tiara

Every princess deserves a crown, right? A delicate tiara or a headband can add a fairytale touch to your persona, making you feel every inch the sissy princess you aspire to be. Select something glittery or floral to maintain that soft, enchanting vibe.

Choosing the Right Handbag

No feminine presentation is complete without the right handbag. It's practical and stylish! Go for handbags in colors that complement your outfit, but don't be afraid to choose something with a little flair—think pastels, sequins, or even a little tassel detail. Remember, your handbag says a lot about you, so choose one that fits your personality and your needs.

The Power of a Perfect Belt

A belt does more than hold up your skirt or trousers—it also defines your waist, creating that desirable hourglass figure. Opt for belts that are medium in width; too thick can overwhelm your frame, and too thin might not make enough of an impact. A lovely cinch around your waist can drastically enhance your silhouette and increase your femininity.

Footwear: The Final Feminine Frontier

Shoes can make or break an outfit. For the sissy princess, think about comfort merged with style—pumps or ballet flats are utterly perfect. They're chic, cute, and elevate your posture and confidence. The right pair of shoes not only ties your outfit together but also affords you the chance to strut with grace and charm.

Let's Not Forget the Small Yet Significant Extras

Finally, consider adding a sprinkle of those often-overlooked accessories like scarves, gloves, or even a stylish pair of glasses. These can introduce new textures and colors to your ensemble, breathing fresh life into your look every day.

Remember, lovelies, choosing the right accessories is all about experimentation and fun. It's your chance to express your inner sissy princess, so go ahead and mix, match, and radiate your fabulous self. With each piece you select, you're crafting the image of the graceful and glamorous femme you're destined to become. Enjoy every moment of your transformation journey—each accessory is a step closer to your ultimate sissy realization.

Feminine Posture and Poise

HELLO THERE, LOVELY! Ready to learn the secrets of feminine posture and poise? Let's embark on this glamorous journey to gracefulness, an essential step in your sissy transformation process!

Importance of Feminine Posture

The way you hold yourself speaks volumes before you even whisper a sweet, "Hello." Feminine posture is not just about standing or sitting but embodies the essence of being perceived as traditionally feminine and elegant. It impacts the way you feel, look, and even the way others perceive you!

Essentials of Feminine Stance

Start with your stance: keep your feet at a slight angle, one foot slightly in front of the other. This stance gives a more delicate and less aggressive appearance than standing squarely on both feet. Distribute your weight mostly on one hip, creating a natural curve in your silhouette, which is a signature in feminine body language.

Sitting Pretty

When sitting, cross your legs at the ankles or knees — both positions enhance a slimmer profile and add a touch of class. Keep your back straight with your shoulders back, but relaxed. Pro tip: think of elongating your body from the pelvis upwards, as if a string is pulling you from the crown of your head.

Walking the Walk

Walking might seem basic, but the way a sissy princess carries herself while walking can turn heads! Let your hips guide you, allowing a natural sway. Small, graceful steps are key here; not only do they look more elegant, they also help in maintaining balance, especially if you're mastering walking in heels.

Arm Movements and Hand Gestures

Avoid stiff arms by your sides. Invite a gentle bend in your elbows, and perhaps carry a small purse or use expressive hand gestures (moderately). Remember, every movement should be smooth and fluid, reflecting the softness traditionally associated with femininity.

Practice Makes Perfect!

Like any skill, mastering feminine posture and poise takes continuous practice. Incorporate these techniques into your daily routine, practicing in front of a mirror whenever possible.

Embrace Your Unique Style

Lastly, while these tips are here to guide you, they are not strict rules. Every individual has their unique style and charisma that they bring to their presentation. Feel free to adapt these suggestions in ways that feel genuine to you, allowing your fabulous sissy personality to shine through!

Remember, darling, the journey to becoming a sissy princess isn't just about looking the part; it's about embodying the poise and confidence that come with your newfound posture. So keep your chin up (literally and figuratively!) and strut gracefully into your fabulous sissy future. You're doing wonderfully!

Chapter 3: Voice and Communication

Feminizing Your Voice

Hello, lovely! Ready to explore transforming your voice into something that feels as fabulous and feminine as you aspire to be? Well, buckle up, because we're diving into the enchanting world of voice feminization. This journey is not only rewarding but also essential in expressing your true sissy princess self. It's all about aligning your voice with your identity, and I'm here to guide you through it with ease and fun!

1. Understand the Basics of Voice Feminization

Voice feminization refers to altering your voice to sound more traditionally feminine. This usually involves working on the pitch, resonance, and intonation of your voice. Remember that women's voices naturally vary, so we're aiming for a softer and more melodic tone that feels right for you.

2. Start with Pitch

Pitch is often the first aspect people try to change when feminizing their voice. A common misconception is thinking you need to speak in a high pitch. Instead, aim for a higher pitch than your usual voice but still within a comfortable range. Use apps or a tuner to practice hitting notes steadily and smoothly.

3. Focus on Resonance

Resonance might be trickier than pitch. It's about where the voice vibrates in your body. Masculine voices typically resonate in the chest, while feminine voices resonate more in the head. Practice speaking from your mouth or nose to achieve a lighter, airier sound.

4. Work on Your Intonation

Intonation is about the melody of your speech. Women tend to have more dynamic intonations, so try varying your tone to convey emotions and questions. It adds expressiveness and a feminine touch to your voice.

5. Practical Exercises to Try

- Humming: Hum in a smooth, high tone to help move your resonance upwards.

- The Lip Trill: This exercise can loosen up your vocal cords and help you reach higher pitches.

- Read Aloud: Pick a passage from your favorite book and read it aloud, experimenting with different pitches and resonances.

6. Lifestyle Changes

Hydration is key! Drink plenty of water as it's great for your vocal cords. Avoid smoking, which can harm your voice. Consider speaking gently and reduce shouting or other vocal strains.

7. Continuous Learning and Practice

Like any other skill, voice training requires consistent practice. Set aside time each day for voice exercises. Record your practice sessions to track your progress and make adjustments.

Remember, feminizing your voice is a personal and unique journey. It should be enjoyable and affirming. You might face some challenges along the way, but stay patient and persistent. With practice, you'll find yourself speaking in a way that truly reflects your sassy and fabulous self!

Embarking on this vocal journey can be one of the most empowering steps you take in your feminization training. Go at your own pace, use these tips as your toolkit, and most importantly, have fun with it. Voice feminization is not just about sounding different; it's about expressing the real, beautiful you. Keep shining, sissy princess!

Speech Patterns and Vocabulary

HEY THERE, LOVELY! Welcome to the delightful exploration of speech patterns and vocabulary that will assist you in your exciting journey of feminization. If you're ready to sprinkle a little more sparkle into your everyday interactions, then you're in the perfect place. Let's turn your communication skills into a magic wand that paints every word you speak with shades of sissy princess charm!

It's All in the Tone! ◈

First up, let's talk about tone. The tone of your voice can convey much more than just the words you choose—it's the secret sauce that can bring your sissy persona to life! Aim for a higher pitch but keep it natural; think gentle, persuasive, and undeniably feminine. Picture your favorite female characters from movies or series – isn't their tone captivating? That's your target!

Mirror, Mirror on the Wall ◈

Practice makes perfect, darling! Recording your voice as you speak and then listening to it can provide you with some real insights. Are your words flowing like a gentle stream or do they need some smoothing over? This exercise isn't just about reaching the right pitch but also about infusing warmth and friendliness into your voice.

Word Play – Choose Wisely ◈

Now, let's sparkle up your vocabulary! Switching up some of your words can add that essential feminine touch to your language. Use softer, more polite forms of expressions. Instead of "okay," why not say "certainly" or "of course"? Such little tweaks can make your speech sound more refined and sissy-appropriate.

Pronunciation is Key ◈

Clear pronunciation is crucial. It adds credibility and charm to your words. Spend some time on pronunciation exercises specifically aimed at softening and feminizing your speech. It's not just about what you say, but how you say it. Graceful, clear, and deliberate pronunciation will make your communication ever so alluring.

The Art of Conversation ◈

Engaging in conversations that typically interest ladies can be quite beneficial. Talk about fashion, arts, or even share some classic recipes. This doesn't mean you should shy away from other topics, but thriving in these areas can significantly enhance your feminine persona.

Practice, Practice, Practice! ◈

Finally, remember that the more you practice, the more natural your feminine speech and vocabulary will become. Chat with friends who support your journey, join online communities, or engage in role plays that encourage you to use your new skills. Every conversation is a chance to excel!

Navigating the nuances of feminization in communication is thrilling and utterly fulfilling. Keep at it, embrace each step of the journey, and remember, each word you learn and each tone shift you master is paving the path to your dream of becoming a sissy princess. Shine on! ◈

Listening Like a Lady

HEY THERE, LOVELY! ◈ Today, we're diving into one of the most graceful arts you can master on your journey to becoming a sissy princess - the art of listening. Yes, darling, how you listen can say as much about your femininity as your voice does. So, let's transform those listening habits to match your fabulous new self!

1. Embrace Empathy:

First up, let's talk empathy. Feminine communication often revolves around understanding and relating to others' emotions. When someone is speaking, try to really feel what they are expressing, beyond just the words. This sensitivity not only endears you to others but enhances your girlish charm.

2. Nod and Smile:

In your interactions, a simple nod and a gentle smile can go a long way. These small gestures show that you are engaged and appreciate the conversation. They are like the silent cheers of communication, encouraging the other person to open up more while presenting you as warm and approachable.

3. Eye Contact:

Maintaining soft, but attentive eye contact shows confidence and respect for the speaker. It's like saying, "I see you, and you're important to me," without uttering a word. Just remember, the goal here is gentle eye engagement, not an intense stare-off!

4. Mind Your Responses:

When it's your turn to respond, keep your tone soft and considerate. Use phrases like "I understand," or "Tell me more," which demonstrate compassion and interest. This doesn't just apply to in-person chats but also to how you interact online or over the phone.

5. Practice Active Listening:

Active listening involves fully concentrating on the speaker, understanding their message, responding thoughtfully, and then remembering what was said. This skill requires practice but is essential for mastering feminine communication. Why not try this during your next outing or even in daily conversations with friends?

6. Avoid Interrupting:

A true lady knows when to pause and let others express themselves fully before she speaks. Interrupting can appear rude and might suggest that your thoughts are more important than theirs. Allow conversations to flow naturally; this patience is a sign of respect and self-control.

7. Softening Your Tone:

Lastly, as you focus on listening like a lady, pay attention to the softness of your voice when you do speak. A gentle, melodic tone can be very disarming and endearing.

By embracing these tips, you'll not only enhance your sissy persona but also build deeper, more meaningful connections with those around you. Remember, communication is about exchanging energy, and as you radiate femininity, you'll attract the same warmth and gentleness in return.

So, go ahead, practice these steps, and let every conversation reflect your inner sissy princess. You've got this! ◈

Art of Feminine Conversation

HELLO, GORGEOUS! ARE you ready to dive into the mellifluous world of feminine conversation? Speaking as a lady might seem like a daunting task, but worry not! This chapter is your friendly guide to mastering the art of sissy talk, making sure you shine in social settings as the sissy princess you aspire to be.

Get Your Tone Right

The foundation of feminine conversation lies in your tone. A softer, higher-pitched voice is often perceived as more feminine. Practice by reading aloud in a slightly higher register than your natural speaking voice. Don't push it too high—aim for natural and sweet. Importantly, keep your tone warm and inviting, as it's all about making your listener feel welcome and engaged.

Focus on Language and Word Choice

Feminine speech often surrounds the use of polite and refined language. Phrases like "Could you kindly" and "If you don't mind" should become staples in your conversation toolkit. Also, sprinkle your sentences with more descriptive adjectives to enhance the softness of your dialogue. Words like 'lovely', 'wonderful', and 'fabulous' add a touch of grace and can transform your conversations.

The Art of Listening

Being a good listener is often more important than being a talker. Show genuine interest in what others are saying by nodding affirmatively and maintaining eye contact. Reflect back what you've heard by saying things like, "That sounds exciting!" or "Tell me more about it." This not only shows that you are listening but also encourages further conversation.

Practicing Compassionate Speech

As a sissy princess, your conversation should be laced with empathy and understanding. Practice phrases that show your compassionate side. For example, responding with "I can imagine how that must feel" or "What can I do to help?" shows empathy and builds a deeper connection with your audience.

Small Talk Mastery

Mastering small talk is essential. Begin with topics everyone can relate to, like the weather, or compliment something they're wearing. Remember, small talk is a gentle warm-up to more engaging dialogues, so keep it light and polite.

Handling Conversations with Grace

No matter what the topic, always handle the conversation with poise and dignity. Avoid slangs or offensive language, maintaining a gentle and lady-like demeanor even when expressing disagreement. A simple "I see your point, but here's what I think..." can express difference without discord.

Regular Practice

Like any other skill, excelling in feminine conversation requires regular practice. Engage in daily conversations, perhaps starting with chats with friends or even practicing in front of a mirror. Record your voice to monitor your progress and make necessary adjustments.

Congratulations on completing this section on the art of feminine conversation! By following these tips and regularly engaging with your training, you'll soon find yourself more confident in your ability to converse femininely, making every social interaction as enchanting as can be. Keep practicing, stay fabulous, and let your sissy princess shine through every word you utter!

Non-verbal Communication Skills

HEY THERE, GORGEOUS! Welcome to one of the most fun and pivotal parts of your sissy transformation journey—mastering the art of non-verbal communication. Whether you're batting those lashes or gracefully moving through a room, the way you communicate without words can speak volumes about your newfound femininity. Let's dive into the subtle yet powerful world of non-verbal cues that will crown you as the enchanting sissy princess you aspire to be!

1. Posture Perfection:

First things first, let's talk about posture. A sissy princess doesn't slouch. It's all about poise and grace. Keep your back straight and your shoulders back but relaxed. When sitting, crossing your legs at the ankles can add that touch of demure elegance. This posture not only makes you look confident but also feels wonderfully feminine.

2. The Art of Walking:

Sashay away! Your walk can tell the world about your sassy and sweet sides. Practice walking with one foot in front of the other, as if on a tightrope, to achieve that alluring hip sway. Remember, it's not about speed but about the soft, fluid motions that define the elegance of a sissy princess.

3. Hand Gestures:

Hands can convey a lot about your character. Use them delicately—whether you're talking, walking, or just sitting still. A soft touch, a gentle wave, and playful twirls of your hair can enhance your feminine allure. Avoid abrupt or rigid movements as they can detract from the softness you want to project.

4. Eye Contact and Facial Expressions:

Master the power of your gaze. Maintaining gentle, yet confident eye contact can draw people in and hold their attention. Pair this with subtle facial expressions—small smiles, surprised looks, and bashful glances can make your interactions more engaging and heartfelt.

5. The Power of Silence:

Sometimes, what you don't say speaks louder than words. Pausing before responding, or simply nodding thoughtfully, can add an air of sophistication to your persona. It's also a great trick to give you a moment to gather your thoughts.

6. Attire and Accessories Influence:

Never underestimate the impact of a well-chosen outfit and complementary accessories! They are your non-verbal cues to the world. Choose colors and styles that reflect your personality and fit the look you are aiming for. From the soft rustle of your dress to the clinking of your bracelets, each element adds to the story you want to tell.

Practice these skills daily, lovely! Each step forward is a step closer to embodying the sissy princess dream. If you ever feel discouraged, remember that each small effort contributes to a big transformation. Radiate confidence, embrace your femininity, and let your non-verbal cues do the talking. See you at the top, sissy princess!

Chapter 4: Behavioral Adjustments

Cultivating Feminine Manners

Hello, lovely! ◈ Welcome to a delightful part of your journey—cultivating those irresistibly feminine manners. In this section, we dive into the subtle yet profound art of femininity that goes beyond clothes and makeup. It's all about molding your behavior to match your radiant sissy princess self. Let's chat about transforming your manners and making your movements as graceful as a ballet dancer!

1. The Art of Politeness

First things first, politeness is key! A true sissy princess knows the power of 'please,' 'thank you,' and 'you're welcome.' It's not just about using these phrases but making them an ingrained part of your interaction with others. Eye contact, a warm smile, and a gentle nod also play pivotal roles in effecting charm and graciousness in every encounter.

2. Voice Modulation

Next up is your voice. The goal? Soft, gentle, and melodic—like a soothing tune that calms and reassures. Practice speaking in a higher pitch but focus on keeping it natural and not forced. Think about the flow of your words; a calm, steady pace reflects confidence and femininity. Excited? Let's not forget the giggles—light and airy!

3. Posture and Movement

Now, let's talk about the way you carry yourself. Picture elegance and you are halfway there! Maintain a straight back with shoulders lightly pulled back. Avoid slouching at all costs—it hides your fabulous self! When seated, cross your legs at the ankles or knees, aligning them gently to one side—pure elegance!

4. Hand Gestures

Hands can speak volumes about you! Keep your movements graceful and deliberate, whether you're sipping tea or simply gesturing in a conversation. Avoid abrupt or large motions that might seem more aggressive than alluring.

5. Walking the Walk

Walking might seem basic, but it's a critical component of your feminine allure. The aim is a smooth, gliding walk—not too fast, each step deliberate. Think about balancing a book on your head! Heels can help cultivate this practice, starting with lower heights and working your way up as you become more comfortable.

6. Dining with Elegance

Mealtime is showtime! Here's where your polished manners truly shine. Learn the proper use of utensils, keeping your elbows off the table, and taking small, delicate bites. Oh, and sipping—not gulping—your drink.

7. Social Graces

Finally, your interaction in social settings. Be attentive, listen more than you speak, and sprinkle your conversations with compliments that are genuine. Understanding the flow of dialogue, knowing when to speak, and when to listen, are keys to mastering social exchanges.

By folding these polished manners into your daily life, you're not just performing; you're transforming. Practice consistently, lovely. It's less about perfect execution and more about the journey of embracing your sissy princess self.

Ready to charm the world? Let's keep sparkling, one graceful step at a time! ◈

Learning to Move Gracefully

HEY THERE, LOVELY! Welcome to one of the most exciting parts of your sissy transformation journey—learning to move gracefully. Movement can say a lot about a person, and adopting a more feminine gait and posture not only helps you look the part but also feel it deep within. So, slip into your favorite heels (if you have them), and let's sway through the basics of feminine grace.

1. Posture is Everything

First things first, a good posture is critical. It's not just about standing up straight; it's about embodying elegance in your stance. Imagine there's a string pulling you from the top of your head, elongating your spine and slightly lifting your chin. Roll those shoulders back gently and let your arms hang naturally by your sides. A good posture will not only make you look taller and more confident but will also give you an air of sophistication.

2. The Art of Walking

Walking in a more traditionally feminine way can be quite different from what you might be used to. Start by placing one foot in front of the other, as if walking along a tightrope. This helps create that hip sway that is often associated with feminine movements. Keep your steps light and your knees slightly bent. Remember, the key here is smoothness and control—no rushing!

3. Sitting Down Gracefully

Sitting down with grace is an art that complements your elegant persona. When you sit, aim to gently lower yourself into the seat, keeping your back straight and your legs together. Once seated, cross your legs at the ankles or knees, depending on what feels most comfortable and natural for you. This position is not only classy but also helps maintain an aura of polished femininity.

4. Hand and Arm Gestures

Your hands and arms offer subtle cues about your femininity. Practice using softer, more fluid gestures when you speak or interact with objects. Avoid abrupt or jerky movements as they can detract from the gentle persona you're embodying. When you're not using your hands, keep them elegantly placed in your lap or gracefully by your side.

5. Practice Makes Perfect

Transforming your movement won't happen overnight—it takes practice. Spend a few minutes each day walking back and forth in a comfortable space, sitting down and standing up, or simply moving around your home. Record yourself if possible, and critique your own movements gently. What would make them more fluid, more refined, more authentically you?

Remember, every step you take on this journey adds to the tapestry of your transformation. Embrace each moment of learning and be proud of your progress. Soon, moving gracefully will become second nature, and you'll dazzle everyone with your poise and elegance.

And there we have it! Integrating these tips into your daily routine will not only help you move more femininely but will genuinely enhance your sissy transformation. Keep practicing, stay confident, and most importantly, enjoy every step of this beautiful journey. You're doing wonderfully, darling!

Now, strut your stuff like the sissy princess you are destined to be!

◇

Girlish Gestures to Incorporate

HELLO, DARLING! ARE you ready to sprinkle a little more femininity into your day with some enchanting girlish gestures? Perfecting the art of feminine movements can significantly enhance your transformation journey in becoming a mesmerizing sissy princess. In this section, we'll delve into the finesse of adopting behaviors and gestures that are traditionally viewed as more feminine, helping you embody the delicate grace that comes with your sissy persona.

Why Focus on Feminine Gestures?

Mastering girlish gestures isn't just about how you look; it's about how you feel and how others perceive you. Each sway of your hips, each flutter of your eyelashes, speaks volumes about your commitment to embracing your sissy identity. Feminine gestures can make you appear more approachable, expressive, and confident in your skin, truly vivifying the sissy princess within!

Let's Begin with the Basics:

1. The Sway Walk: Practice walking with one foot in front of the other, letting your hips gently sway side-to-side. This walk not only enhances feminine charm but also helps you develop balance and elegance in heels.

2. Hand Gestures: Females often use softer hand movements. Practice moving your hands fluidly, with slight gestures during conversation. Avoid harsh or sudden movements that can appear less graceful.

3. The Art of Sitting: Always cross your legs at the ankles or knees when sitting. This posture is not only seen as traditionally feminine but also helps maintain a modest and refined appearance.

4. Expressive Facial Reactions: Learning to express emotions through your facial expressions can make interactions more engaging. Practice reactions like a soft smile, a gentle furrow of eyebrows, and wide-eyed wonderment to enhance your expressive communication.

5. Voice Modulation: Adopting a softer, higher-pitched voice can significantly affect how your femininity is perceived. Spend some time each day practicing your voice tone, focusing on maintaining a gentle melodic quality.

Integrating Gestures into Daily Practice:

To truly incorporate these gestures into your everyday behavior, consistent practice is key. Start by choosing one gesture at a time and focus on mastering it throughout the week. Record videos of yourself performing everyday tasks with these new gestures, analyze them, and make improvements.

Remember, girlish gestures are about adding layers of subtlety and grace to your persona. It's not about overdoing it but finding the right balance that aligns with your identity as a sissy princess.

Challenges and How to Overcome Them:

Adopting new behaviors can initially feel awkward or unnatural. If you find yourself struggling, take a step back and remind yourself why you started this journey. Reconnect with your goals, and maybe even reach out to the community for support and guidance.

By incorporating these girlish gestures into your daily life, you're not just learning new behaviors but are also crafting a whole new aura of femininity that will transform your presence. Remember, every step forward is a step closer to your fabulous goal of becoming a sissy princess. So keep practicing, stay dedicated, and most importantly, have fun with your transformation!

Share your progress, questions, or any fabulous tips you've discovered along the way in the comment section below or on our social media platforms. Each bit of shared experience builds us all up stronger!

Emotional Expressiveness

HEY THERE, LOVELY! If you're diving deep into your sissy transformation journey, one critical aspect you won't want to overlook is cultivating your Emotional Expressiveness. Let's talk about why this is essential and how you can enhance it to enrich your sissy persona.

Becoming a sissy isn't just about the outward appearance; it's equally about internal transformation. Emotional expressiveness is about letting your feelings show and connecting with your more feminine, expressive side. This doesn't just mean being more open or emotional; it means fine-tuning your expressiveness to resonate with the sissy identity you are embracing.

Why It Matters?

Emotions are powerful. They can be your greatest strength if you understand and express them well. For a sissy, mastering emotional expressiveness is crucial because it helps in achieving a deeper level of femininity that goes beyond physical appearance. When you engage with your emotions openly and authentically, you embody the essence of being not just a sissy but a sissy princess.

Start with Self-Reflection

First and foremost, get in touch with your own emotions. Spend time understanding what you feel and why. Keeping a journal can be a fabulous way to start. Write down your thoughts and emotions daily. This will not only help you understand your emotional pattern but also improve your emotional literacy.

Learn the Art of Empathy

To express emotions well, you'll need to understand the feelings of others also. Being empathetic allows you to connect with people on a deeper level, making your interactions more meaningful and your persona more relatable and likable. Try to genuinely put yourself in other people's shoes and understand their perspectives and feelings.

Expressing with Your Whole Self

Expression isn't just verbal; it's also about your body language, your facial expressions, and even your tone of voice. Practice in front of a mirror, watch films or shows with expressive characters, and try mimicking them. Pay attention to how they move their hands, how they look while feeling different emotions, and how their voice changes with their moods.

Enhancing Your Vocabulary

Sometimes, we fail to express our emotions because we simply don't have the words. Expanding your emotional vocabulary can help you better articulate your feelings. Learn new words and phrases that describe emotions and practice using them in sentences about how you feel.

Engage in Artistic Expression

Art can be a sanctuary for those cultivating their emotional expressiveness. Whether it's drawing, writing poetry, dancing, or even crafting, these activities offer unique pathways for exploring and expressing your emotions. They allow an outlet for your feelings and foster creativity, adding depth to your sissy transformation.

Feedback and Adjust

Finally, don't shy away from seeking feedback. Talk to friends or fellow sissies about how you're expressing yourself. Getting another's perspective can be incredibly helpful. They can offer insights into how you come across and suggest tweaks to make your emotions come through more clearly or appropriately.

So, darling, remember, emotional expressiveness is a journey. It's all about finding ways to let your inner sissy shine through sincerely and vividly. Dive into these practices with an open heart, and you'll soon find yourself blossoming into the sissy princess you aspire to be! Keep fluttering those lashes with genuine emotion, and let your heartfelt expressions paint your interactions in the most delightful hues.

Politeness and Etiquette

WELCOME TO A CRUCIAL section of our delightful journey into feminization training. As we dive into the intricacies of politeness and etiquette, remember that embodying the grace of a sissy princess is about more than just looks – it's about behavior too! Here, we'll explore and refine the subtle arts of manners and interaction, transforming you into the epitome of politeness and femininity.

1. Mastering the Art of Greetings

Every interaction begins with a greeting, making it the golden opportunity to set a dainty, feminine tone. Practice a soft, friendly tone of voice; it's about making the other person feel welcomed and appreciated. Whether it's a simple "Hello" or a cheerful "Good morning," make sure your greeting sounds gentle yet joyful.

2. Conversation Flow

Engage in conversations with grace and active listening. Show genuine interest by asking thoughtful questions, nodding, and maintaining eye contact. Remember, a sissy princess avoids interrupting and speaks thoughtfully. When it's your turn to talk, keep your voice modulated and your topics polite and pleasant.

3. Table Manners

Whether it's a casual meal or a formal dinner, table manners speak volumes about your femininity. Learn the proper use of utensils, and remember, small bites and slow eating rate are key. Keep your posture upright––no elbows on the table––and place your napkin on your lap. Your elegance at the table should make a lasting impression.

4. Dressing Appropriately

Attire is a critical component of your etiquette. Dressing according to the occasion says a lot about your respect for the event and its attendees. For your sissy transformation, focus on clean, well-fitted, and situation-appropriate outfits that enhance your femininity. Always ensure that your clothing choices reflect a polished and immaculate style.

5. Polite Departures

Parting is as important as meeting. Always leave on a sweet note with a polite "Thank you for your company" or "It was wonderful spending time with you." A graceful goodbye, possibly with a light, friendly hug or a cheek kiss, depending on the context and your relationship with the person, seals your interaction beautifully.

6. Handling Conflicts with Grace

Even in uncomfortable situations, a sissy princess remains composed. When faced with conflicts, respond with patience and keep your tone soft but assertive when necessary. Avoid raising your voice or making quick judgments. Offering a polite excuse to step away from a heated situation can often save both face and grace.

Essential Tips:

- Always carry a few femininity props like a small handkerchief or a delicate fan; they can add flair to your mannerisms and serve practical purposes.

- Rehearse phrases like "Please," "Thank you", and "You're welcome." These are your go-to expressions for maintaining a persona of politeness.

- Reflect frequently on your behavior and adjust as required. Consider keeping a journal to track your progress in manners and etiquette.

The journey to absolute sissification is rich with learning and adopting exquisite mannerisms. Politeness and etiquette are not just behaviors but an integral part of your new identity. Seamlessly blending these qualities into your daily interactions will help cement your status as a true sissy princess, radiating charm and gentility wherever you go. Enjoy this transformative venture, as each step brings you closer to the elegant essence of femininity.

Chapter 5: Sissy Role Models and Inspiration

Iconic Feminine Figures

When embarking on your journey of feminization, finding the right role models can be incredibly inspiring. In this section, we'll dive deep into the world of iconic feminine figures who embody elegance, grace, and strength. These are not just celebrities but paragons of feminine virtues that you, as an aspiring sissy princess, can look up to and emulate.

Embrace Elegance: Audrey Hepburn

Audrey Hepburn isn't just a symbol of classic beauty and elegance, she's a beacon of grace that transcends time. Audrey's style, poise, and kindness make her a perfect role model for anyone looking to embody classic femininity. Study her films, not just for her flawless style, but for her body language and demeanor, which exude femininity and sophistication.

Channel Boldness: Madonna

Madonna is the epitome of boldness and reinvention, constantly evolving her style and music while staying unequivocally feminine. For a sissy looking to capture some of Madonna's fearless spirit, look at her fearless fashion choices and her ability to command attention. The key lesson here? Never be afraid to express your femininity in bold and unconventional ways.

Learn Resilience: Oprah Winfrey

Oprah Winfrey's journey from humble beginnings to becoming a media mogul is a powerful story of resilience. Oprah's strength and wisdom make her a great role model for sissies aiming to overcome challenges. Her interviews and speeches are goldmines for learning how to communicate effectively and connect with others on an emotional level.

Seek Compassion: Princess Diana

Known for her compassion and humanitarian work, Princess Diana was not only a royal but a global icon of kindness and care. Her ability to empathize with people from all walks of life and her commitment to making the world a better place are qualities every sissy can aspire to. Emulating her compassion can help you foster deeper connections in your sissy journey.

Cultivate Mystery: Marlene Dietrich

Marlene Dietrich, known for her allure and mystery, was a German actress and singer who challenged traditional gender roles with her fashion and film choices. Her blend of masculine and feminine styles, along with her mesmerizing performances, make her a fascinating figure for any sissy looking to add an element of intrigue to their persona.

Through studying these iconic feminine figures, you can draw a wealth of knowledge and inspiration. Incorporate their unique qualities into your sissy transformation by adopting their attitudes, mimicking their style, or living by their principles. Remember, while these women provide a fantastic blueprint, the essence of your journey is about creating an authentic version of yourself that resonates with these timeless attributes of femininity.

Contemporary Sissy Icons

HEY THERE, LOVELY! If you're diving into the sissy lifestyle, finding some modern sissy icons can provide both inspiration and a splash of glam to your transformation journey. These icons are not just about their looks; they embody the confidence and courage that align with embracing one's sissy identity fully. Let's get to know a few shining stars in the contemporary sissy scene who can light the way for your own fabulous journey.

1. Conchita Wurst

When talking about breaking boundaries, Conchita Wurst stands out brilliantly. Rising to fame after winning the Eurovision Song Contest in 2014, Conchita, with her bearded diva persona, became a global symbol of inclusivity and gender fluidity. She shows us that femininity can come with 0, 1, or 100 beards – it's all about how you wear your identity with pride!

2. Jinkx Monsoon

For fans of the drag scene, Jinkx Monsoon, winner of RuPaul's Drag Race Season 5, is a phenomenal role model. Jinkx is known not only for her incredible talent as a performer but also for her candidness about her gender identity. Embracing the fluidity of gender, Jinkx represents the playful and transformative nature of the sissy lifestyle, reminding us that at the end of the day, our identity is indeed a beautiful play of self-expression.

3. Kim Chi

Another RuPaul's Drag Race alumni, Kim Chi, celebrates her sissy identity with a bold and artistic approach to femininity. Her makeup skills are nothing short of visionary, turning each appearance into an avant-garde expression of softness paired with strength. Kim Chi encourages all sissies to find their unique style and to embrace the artistry in their feminization journey.

4. Gigi Gorgeous

A true icon in the transgender community, Gigi Gorgeous has documented her transition and life on YouTube, providing a real-life glimpse into the joys and challenges faced on the path to self-realization. Gigi's story is not just about becoming a woman, but about becoming oneself unapologetically. She stands as a beacon for anyone navigating their own transformations, promoting a message of self-love and authenticity.

5. Laverne Cox

As an acclaimed actress and an outspoken advocate for transgender rights, Laverne Cox has carved out a space for transgender individuals in the mainstream media. Her role in "Orange Is the New Black" broke significant barriers and her advocacy work continues to promote important conversations about inclusivity and rights. Laverne's visibility and success inspire sissies to aspire and achieve in all areas of life, not just in personal transformation.

Exploring the lives and careers of these icons can enrich your journey by offering diverse perspectives on what it means to live authentically in a sissy role. Each of these figures teaches us something unique about courage, self-acceptance, and the art of transformation. Allow their stories to influence and inspire your own path, and remember, every sissy journey is as unique as the individual walking it. Shine on, and let your sissy flag wave high and proud, inspired by these magnificent contemporary sissy icons!

Learning from Fictional Sissy Characters

HELLO, MY FABULOUS reader! In this exciting part of our journey, let's dive into the enchanting world of fictional sissy characters. These characters often embody the elegance, grace, and challenges of embracing one's sissy persona, making them wonderful guides and sources of inspiration on your enchanting journey to becoming a sissy princess.

Fictional characters, whether in books, movies, or TV shows, can be more than just entertainment. They hold the power to inspire and instruct, providing insights into the complexities and joys of sissy transformation. Each character's story and experiences can offer unique lessons and tips that might resonate with your own journey.

Why Learn from Fictional Sissy Characters?

1. Empathy and Relatability: Often, these characters go through emotional and transformational journeys that you might find relatable.

Observing their responses to various situations can help you understand and manage your feelings and reactions in similar circumstances.

2. Learning Through Observation: Watching or reading about a character's transformation allows you to visualize what certain aspects of being a sissy entail, including both the struggles and triumphs. It's like having a roadmap that highlights the peaks and pits you might encounter.

3. Inspiration and Motivation: Seeing a character embrace their sissy identity with confidence can be immensely motivating. It's a reminder of the joys and self-acceptance that await you on the other side of your transformation.

4. Fashion and Style Tips: Fictional sissy characters are often dressed stunningly, which gives you ample opportunity to take notes on fashion. From fabulous frocks to exquisite accessories, these characters can be your style gurus.

Iconic Fictional Sissy Characters to Learn From

Let's examine some beloved sissy characters from fiction and discuss what we can learn from each:

- Character from Movie/Show 1: Here's your first glam icon. Let's analyze their story arc—how they accepted their identity, the obstacles they faced, and how they overcame them. Notice their interactions, their wardrobe choices, and how they express themselves. Each of these elements provides layers of learning and inspiration.

- Character from Book 2: This character offers a more introspective journey into the sissy transformation. Reading allows you to get into their thoughts, understand their internal conflicts, and celebrate their moments of self-acceptance. Look for passages that resonate with your feelings or aspirations.

- Character from TV Show 3: Perfect for observing day-to-day sissyness within a broader societal context. How does the character deal with public perception? What strategies do they employ to feel fabulous and fearless in everyday situations?

How to Incorporate These Lessons into Your Journey

1. Journaling: After watching a movie or reading about a character, jot down the traits or actions you admire. Could you see yourself adopting any of their styles or attitudes? How would these changes make you feel?

2. Role-playing: Occasionally, step into the shoes of your favorite characters. This doesn't mean imitating them blindly, but rather, borrowing elements that you feel enhance your sissy persona.

3. Creating a Vision Board: If visual motivation works for you, clip pictures or quotes from these characters and build a vision board. This can be a powerful visualization tool that keeps you inspired.

4. Discussion Groups or Forums: Engage with communities that discuss these characters. Sharing interpretations and feelings with like-minded individuals can offer new insights and bolster your journey.

Remember, while fictional characters provide wonderful templates and ideas, your sissy transformation is uniquely yours. Borrow what sparks joy and resonates with your personal aspirations, and tailor these influences to suit your journey.

Stay fabulous and stay inspired, for every page you turn and every show you watch could have that magic spark to propel your transformation towards becoming a sissy princess! Let these fictional mentors guide you, comfort you, and above all, inspire you to be unapologetically you.

Role Model Case Studies

HEY THERE, LOVELY! As you embark on your enchanting journey to becoming a sissy princess, it's crucial to have some shining examples to guide your way. In this section, we'll dive into some heartwarming and inspiring case studies of individuals who have successfully embraced their sissy personas. These stories are not just tales; they're blueprints that can help you navigate your own path of feminization training with grace and excitement!

Embracing the Sparkle: Jessica's Journey

Meet Jessica. She started her journey much like you, curious and a bit unsure. But with dedication, she transformed her life and now lives every day to its fullest as a sissy princess. Jessica's secret? Immersing herself in the community, learning from others, and never skipping her training assignments. She found that attending themed dress-up events and participating in online forums boosted her confidence immensely.

From Shy to Showstopper: Tim's Transformation

Next, let's talk about Tim, or as she prefers, Tiffany. Tiffany was once incredibly shy and reserved, struggling to express her true self. Her breakthrough came when she realized that being a sissy wasn't just about the clothes and makeup; it was about expressing her inner femininity and connecting with like-minded souls. Her advice? Start small—maybe with a pair of cute socks or a pretty scarf—and gradually step up to more elaborate attire as you grow more comfortable.

Persistence Pays: Alex's Adventures

Alex's story is all about persistence. Initial setbacks and a lack of support from peers could have easily discouraged him, but Alex kept at his dreams, educated himself thoroughly through materials like ours, and attended workshops. Now, Alex proudly shares his journey at conferences as an example of how persistence can lead you to your ultimate goal of sissy perfection.

Community and Support: Nina's Network

Lastly, we have Nina, who emphasizes the importance of a supportive community. Nina found her tribe online, where she could share experiences, exchange tips, and even find mentors. She suggests looking for local or virtual groups where you can feel safe and supported throughout your transformation process.

• • ❧ • •

BY LEARNING ABOUT THE journeys of Jessica, Tiffany, Alex, and Nina, you can see that while everyone's path to becoming a sissy princess is unique, there are common threads that bind all their stories: community, persistence, and gradual self-expression. Embrace these lessons, and remember, each step forward, no matter how small, is a step toward achieving your fabulous sissy persona. So, dust off those heels, practice that makeup, and let your sissy princess shine through!

Ready to continue your journey with inspiration from those who've truly embraced their transformation? Let these role models light your path to becoming the sissy princess you are destined to be. Keep flipping through the pages for more tips and assignments that will help you express your truest, most fabulous self!

Creating Your Sissy Persona

STEPPING INTO THE WORLD of feminization can be thrilling, yet overwhelming. One integral step in your journey is crafting your sissy persona. This is more than just an alter ego; it's a deeper expression of your inner self, wrapped in the outward joy of femininity. Think of this process as a fun and creative art project where you are the canvas!

Unleash Your Inner Sissy

First things first, start by asking yourself what type of sissy resonates with you. Are you drawn to the classic, elegant princess type? Or perhaps the flirty, bubbly cheerleader is more your style? Maybe you feel more connected to being a sultry diva or a sweet, demure maid. Knowing who you want to become will guide your transformation.

Choosing Your Name

Choosing a name for your sissy persona is like planting a seed that will grow into your new identity. Pick something that not only sounds appealing but also feels right and has a personal connection. This could be a variation of your favorite female name or something entirely imaginative. Remember, your sissy name will be a significant part of your new identity, so choose wisely!

Dressing the Part

Clothing is a powerful tool in the feminization process. It can accentuate your features and help manifest your persona. Start exploring styles that not only appeal to your personal aesthetic but also flatter your body type. Whether it's skirts, dresses, stockings, or heels, each piece adds a layer to your evolving sissy persona. Don't forget about accessories and makeup – these are the finishing touches that bring your character to life.

Developing Behaviors and Mannerisms

Your journey isn't just about how you look but also how you carry yourself. Observing and incorporating feminine gestures into your behavior can enhance your persona. Pay attention to your speech, the way you walk, sit, and react in interactions. This alignment of your external and internal self helps solidify your sissy persona in the eyes of both yourself and others.

Exploring Your Interests

What does your sissy persona love doing? Maybe she adores baking, dancing, or maybe she's an avid reader. These hobbies not only make your sissy life more interesting but also give you activities to focus on during your transformation process. Plus, they're fantastic opportunities to meet like-minded sissies!

Stay True to Yourself

While it's exciting to explore various aspects of femininity, it's important to stay true to who you are. Your sissy persona should be a reflection of your genuine self, embellished with your feminine aspirations. Embrace your uniqueness and let it shine through your sissy identity.

Embarking on this journey can be incredibly rewarding and fulfilling. Every ribbon tied, every lipstick shade tried, and every step in heels is a step towards discovering the sissy princess within you. Remember, creating your sissy persona is a process – it's okay to experiment, refine, and even start over. With each step, you'll find yourself embracing a more confident and joyous expression of yourself. So, go forth, be bold, and let your sissy flag fly high!

Chapter 6: Fitness and Body Shaping

Exercises for a Sissy Figure

Hello, darling! Welcome to the heart of transforming your physical form - designing that sensuously svelte sissy figure. Whether you're yearning for a more curvaceous silhouette or simply aiming to maintain a petite posture, this section is tailored just for you!

Understanding the Basics: Building a Feminine Physique

Creating a feminine shape revolves around accentuating the classic hourglass figure. This means targeted exercises that enhance the hips and buttocks while slimming the waist. But remember, sweetie, while workouts can reshape and tone your body, embracing who you are and how you look is key to your sissy transformation.

Warm-Ups to Wisp You Away

Begin every workout with gentle stretches. Not only do they prevent injuries, but stretching can also elongate your muscles, contributing to a more slender appearance. Think about grace in each movement — almost like you're performing a slow, flowing dance.

1. The Butterfly Stretch: Sit down, bend your knees, and bring your feet together. Gently push your knees towards the ground using your elbows, holding for about 30 seconds.

2. Waist Pinchers: Excellent for sculpting that desired wasp waist, side bends and torso twists will be your best friends. Ensure fluid, slow movements to maintain the air of femininity.

Cinching That Waist

Any sissy training guide will emphasize a nipped-in waist. It's central to achieving a sissy figure and, frankly, it's where the magic happens!

- **Bicycle Crunches:** Lay on your back and mimic a pedal motion with your legs raised in the air. Touch your elbow to the opposite knee alternatively. Aim for 3 sets of 15 reps.

- **Planks:** Start on your elbows and toes, keeping your back straight. Hold for 20 to 30 seconds, gradually increasing as you get more comfortable.

Boosting Your Bottom

Now, let's pump up those adorable bottom curves with some specific exercises that focus on the buttocks.

- **Squats:** Stand with your feet slightly wider than hip-width apart and squat, keeping your back straight and chest up. For an extra challenge, add a small dumbbell.

- **Glute Bridges:** Lie on your back with your knees bent, feet flat on the ground. Lift your hips while squeezing your glutes, hold for three seconds, and lower slowly.

Final Tips to Keep You Motivated

Sweetheart, the key to any exercise routine is consistency. Make your workouts fun and fabulous by perhaps wearing your favorite outfit or playing uplifting tunes. Remember, each small step you take is crafting the stunning sissy figure you desire. Keep at it, and don't fear embracing the flamboyant, fantastic you at every stretch and bend!

By staying true to your goals, keeping up with your exercises, and always choosing love and acceptance at each step of your journey, you're not just shaping your body; you're molding a fabulous new you. Ready, set, sashay away into your next workout session, you marvelous sissy, you! ⟡

Diet for Skin, Hair, and Nails

HELLO, LOVELY SISSIES! Let's talk about something super important in your journey to becoming the ultimate sissy princess: your diet. What you eat doesn't just affect your waistline, it also plays a crucial role in how your skin glows, how your hair shines, and how strong your nails are—three essentials for looking fabulous!

Glowing Skin

To get that soft, dewy princess skin, hydration is key. Start by drinking plenty of water. Aim for 8-10 glasses a day—hydrated skin is happy skin. Add a splash of lemon for some extra zest and detoxifying benefits!

Foods rich in Omega-3 fatty acids, like flaxseeds, walnuts, and fatty fish (think salmon or mackerel), can boost your skin's health, giving it a radiant glow. Also, vegetables high in antioxidants, like tomatoes and bell peppers, protect your skin from environmental damage.

Lustrous Hair

For hair that glistens under your tiara, focus on biotin-rich foods. Eggs, almonds, and avocados are great choices. These foods help in strengthening your hair and add a natural sheen to it.

Iron and zinc are essential for hair growth and health. Include lean meats, spinach, and lentils into your diet. These nutrients not only help in hair growth but also improve hair thickness and reduce breakage.

Strong Nails

Your hands express your femininity, so strong, well-manicured nails are a must. For stronger nails, incorporate more protein into your diet—think chicken, tofu, and beans. Biotin also plays a key role here, so those almonds and eggs will double-benefit your nails and hair!

Calcium is another crucial component for nail strength. Include calcium-rich foods like yogurt, cheese, and green leafy vegetables in your meals. Additionally, a bit of vitamin D (from the sun or supplements) ensures that your body absorbs all that good calcium effectively.

Tips for Incorporating These Foods Into Your Diet

1. Start Your Day Right: A smoothie with spinach, flaxseed oil, and a hand full of berries will kickstart your skin and hair health each morning.

2. Snack Smart: Opt for snacks like yogurt or a handful of nuts. These are not just tasty but are also packed with the good stuff for your hair and nails.

3. Balanced Meals: For lunch and dinner, think half a plate of vegetables, a quarter plate of protein, and a quarter of complex carbohydrates like whole grains. This balance supports all-rounded beauty and health.

4. Stay Consistent: Just like any other training, consistency is key. Regular intake of these foods multiplies their benefits, helping you achieve that princess-like allure.

Embarking on this dietary enrichment plan will help you radiate from within, making your sissy transformation even more spectacular. You'll not only feel healthier, but you'll also shine with that quintessential sissy sparkle—externally and internally!

Stay fabulous and keep feasting on these beautifying treasures, darling! With each bite, you're one step closer to revealing your inner sissy princess. So go ahead, eat your way to stunning!

Feminine Agility and Flexibility

HELLO, GORGEOUS! READY to sprinkle some sparkle into your fitness routine? As we dive into the world of feminine agility and flexibility, remember this isn't just about reshaping your body; it's about empowering you to strut your stuff with confidence and grace!

Why Focus on Flexibility?

First things first, let's talk about why flexibility matters in your sissy transformation journey. Flexibility isn't just for ballerinas and gymnasts — it's a crucial element in adopting a more graceful and feminine posture. It helps in reducing muscle stiffness, increasing range of motion, and most importantly, giving you that delicate, elegant gait that defines sissy poise.

Getting Started with Stretching

Incorporate stretching exercises into your daily routine. Aim for at least 10-15 minutes of dedicated stretching to keep your muscles long, limber, and ready for more advanced feminization fitness assignments. Here are a few stretches to try:

- Butterfly Stretch: Perfect for your inner thighs, hips, and lower back.
- Cat-Cow Stretch: Great for spine flexibility and abdominal control.
- Seated Leg Stretch: Targets your hamstrings and enhances leg flexibility.

Remember, each stretch should be held gently for 15-30 seconds to benefit most from it.

Yoga: A Secret Weapon

Yoga isn't just another workout; it's a transformative practice that aligns your body, mind, and spirit. Here are a few yoga poses that emphasize grace and flexibility:

- Tree Pose: Enhances balance and strengthens your core, helping you achieve that svelte, sissy silhouette.
- Warrior II: Opens up your hips and chest, an excellent pose for building shape and stamina.
- Cobra Pose: This gentle backbend is fabulous for tightening your glutes and gives you a stretch down the front of your body.

Incorporate Dance Movements

Dance isn't just fun — it's a fantastic way to build the sissy fluidity and elegance you're aiming for. Ballet, in particular, is marvelous for this, but any form of dance that encourages delicate, flowing movements will do wonders for your femininity training. Try to include at least a few minutes of dance into your daily routine. It could be as simple as moving to a song you love in front of your mirror!

Consistency is Key

Remember, transforming your body into a more feminine form takes time and consistency. Make these exercises a regular part of your lifestyle, and soon, you'll notice significant transformations not only in your flexibility and agility but in your overall femininity as well.

Agility and flexibility training is about more than just looking the part; it's about feeling deeply attuned with your feminized self, moving in ways that feel right and natural to you. Keep pushing your boundaries, keep refining your movements, and most importantly, have fun with it! You're on a beautiful journey, transforming into the sissy princess you aspire to be, and every stretch, every pose brings you closer to that reality.

Impact of Hormones on Body Shaping

HEY THERE, LOVELY SISSY-in-training! As you embark on this transformative journey to become the sissy princess of your dreams, it's important we chat about a topic that can hugely impact your body shaping efforts – hormones. Understanding how hormones can affect your transformation goals not only helps you see clearer results but also guides you in aligning your body shaping strategies effectively.

What Are Hormones, Anyway?

Hormones are like your body's little messengers – they travel through your bloodstream to tissues and organs, helping control and coordinate various body functions. For someone aspiring to feminize their appearance, the focus is mainly on two types: estrogen and testosterone. Estrogen promotes the development of what are traditionally considered feminine physical features, such as breasts and a fuller hip ratio, while testosterone does the opposite.

How Do Hormones Affect Body Shaping?

When you're aiming to enhance feminine traits, managing the balance between estrogen and testosterone is key. Higher levels of estrogen can help distribute fat to typical female areas like your hips, thighs, and buttocks, giving you that desired curvier figure. On the other hand, reducing testosterone levels can slow down or reduce the growth of body hair and may prevent the buildup of muscle mass in areas typical of a masculine physique.

Safe Ways to Adjust Hormones

1. Consult with Medical Professionals: This is Numero Uno! Before you think of starting hormone therapy or any supplement intake, speak with a healthcare provider who's knowledgeable about transgender or feminization health care. They can guide you on safe practices, appropriate doses, and regularly monitor your health.

2. Healthy Lifestyle Choices: While hormones can be adjusted through medical interventions, incorporating a healthy diet and regular exercise that promotes flexibility and endurance, rather than muscle bulk, can complement the effects of hormones. Plus, staying hydrated and getting enough sleep are crucial for maintaining hormone balance.

3. Mind the Side Effects: Hormonal treatment isn't without its risks and side effects, which can range from mood swings and weight gain to more serious health risks. Continuous medical supervision is imperative to navigate these safely.

A Sissy's Tool Kit for Hormone Management

Include in your toolkit:

- Support network: Regular check-ins with your doctor, and maybe conversations with fellow sissies undergoing similar changes, can offer invaluable support.

- Education: Stay informed about the latest research and resources on hormone effects and feminization.

- Patience: Body transformation is a journey, not a sprint. Celebrate small milestones and maintain a positive outlook.

Remember, your transformation into a sissy princess should be a safe, informed, and enjoyable process. By understanding the critical role hormones play in body shaping and taking steps to manage them responsibly, you're on your path to achieving your fabulous goals. Keep shining bright, and embrace each step of your journey with knowledge, caution, and a dash of sparkle! ✧

Maintaining a Healthy Routine

HELLO, GORGEOUS! STAYING active and keeping fit plays a huge part in your transformation journey. Not only does it help sculpt your body into the sissy princess shape you're aiming for, but it also boosts your mood and energy levels, making every step of your feminization process even more sparkling!

Regular Exercise is Key

Make exercise a non-negotiable part of your daily routine. Tailoring a fitness plan that emphasizes areas you want to feminize can create wonders. Activities like yoga, Pilates, and targeted strength training can enhance your lower body curves, tone your legs, and help carve out that desired sissy silhouette. Remember, the goal is to maintain flexibility and develop a more traditionally feminine physique, so focus on exercises that are nurturing and not too harsh on your body.

Healthy Eating Habits

What you eat is just as important as your workout routine. A balanced diet rich in fruits, vegetables, whole grains, and lean proteins will nourish your body and support the changes you're aiming for. Foods that are high in estrogen-like compounds such as soy products can also be beneficial for feminization. However, it's important to consult with a nutritionist to create a diet plan that's tailored to your specific needs and goals.

Consistency is Crucial

Consistency in both diet and exercise is the secret sauce to success. Set yourself up with a daily routine that integrates seamlessly with your lifestyle. It doesn't have to be overwhelming – start with small, manageable changes and gradually build up as you become more comfortable and confident in your capabilities.

Rest and Recovery

Don't forget, rest is just as crucial as action. Your body needs time to recuperate and heal from the physical demands you're placing on it. Ensure you're getting enough sleep and consider incorporating restorative practices such as meditation or deep-breathing exercises into your routine. This not only helps you physically but also ensures that you stay mentally and emotionally balanced, which is integral to your transformation.

Track Your Progress

Keeping a journal or a blog about your fitness journey can be incredibly rewarding and motivating. Document your workouts, what you eat, how you feel, and the changes you're observing. Not only will this help you keep a record of what works best for you, but it will also give you something to look back on and be proud of!

By maintaining a healthy routine, you ensure that every day you're becoming more and more the sissy princess you desire to be. Embrace the journey, love the process, and remember, every step forward is a step towards achieving your fabulous goals. Let's keep moving, darling!

Chapter 7: Developing Feminine Skills

Cooking and Baking

Hello, lovely sissy-in-training! Welcome to one of the most delightful sections of your feminization journey—Cooking and Baking. Embracing your inner domestic goddess is not only a fabulous way to enhance your sissy persona but also a fantastic skill set to enrich your daily life. Let's dive into the sweet and savory world that awaits in your kitchen!

Why Cooking and Baking Matter: Cooking and baking are traditional skills that resonate deeply with feminine energy. They are nurturing, creative, and immensely satisfying. Picture yourself in a cute apron, whipping up delicious treats or a nutritious meal, and you'll see why these activities are perfect for connecting with your sissy self.

Starting Simple: First things first, you don't need to be a gourmet chef overnight. Begin with basic recipes that do not require complicated techniques or exotic ingredients. Think about making a lovely salad, a gorgeous sandwich, or even baking some simple cookies. Each task you master will boost your confidence and inspire you to try more complex dishes.

Creating Your Sissy Cooking Space: Make your kitchen inviting. Perhaps add some pink utensils or a floral apron to set the mood. The ambiance is crucial—remember, you are crafting an experience, not just a meal!

Recipe Selection: Choose recipes that speak to you. Whether it's decadent desserts or hearty main courses, pick dishes that excite you. Cooking is as much about joy as it is about food preparation. Consider starting a recipe diary where you can jot down successful recipes and notes about what you might want to try next.

Presentation Skills: As a sissy, appearance matters! Learn the art of plating. Use colors, garnishes, and beautiful dishware to turn each meal into a visual feast. Remember, we eat with our eyes first!

Cooking with Others: Sharing the kitchen with friends or fellow sissies can be incredibly fun and fulfilling. Plan a cooking day where you can exchange tips, enjoy each other's company, and perhaps even have a mini-feast with all the dishes you prepare together.

Seasonal and Fresh: Embrace the seasons by choosing ingredients that are in season. Not only does this improve the taste of your dishes, but it also connects you more deeply with the world around you. Visit local farmers' markets to find fresh, inspiring ingredients.

Cultural Exploration through Cuisine: Exploring dishes from different cultures can be a fabulous way to widen your culinary horizon and add diverse flavors to your cooking repertoire. Each recipe tells a story, and as a sissy, weaving these stories into your cooking can make every meal an adventure.

Health and Nutrition: While it's fun to indulge, maintaining a balanced diet is essential. Learn about nutritional values and try to incorporate a healthy balance of proteins, carbs, and fats, along with plenty of fruits and vegetables.

Cooking and baking are about more than just food—they're about crafting an experience that delights all senses. Through this journey, you not only enhance your sissy aesthetic but also gain life skills that bring joy and health. So, tie on your prettiest apron, gather your tools, and let's get fabulous in the kitchen! Remember, every mistake is just a learning step towards making you the ultimate sissy princess chef. Bon appétit!

Decorating and Home Management

HELLO DARLINGS! WELCOME to one of the most enjoyable aspects of your sissy transformation journey—mastering the art of decorating and home management. This isn't just about keeping things tidy; it's about creating a space that reflects your sissy princess persona, brimming with charm and femininity. Let's dive into the fluff and fold of feminizing your living space!

1. Embrace Your Inner Interior Designer

First things first, think about what kind of atmosphere you want to evoke in your personal space. Do soft pastels and floral patterns speak to you, or are you more of a shimmer-and-lace kind of sissy? Play with colors and textures that feel right to you. Adding touches like plush cushions, silky throws, and delicate figurines can instantly transform a dull space into a sissy haven.

2. Organizing with Elegance

Organization is key to maintaining your newly decorated haven. Start by decluttering—yes, it might be hard to let go of things, but keeping only what you truly need or love makes space for your new sissy items. Use pretty boxes and baskets to store your essentials. Not only will they keep things organized, but they also add to the decor!

3. Master the Art of Scent

Scent can dramatically affect the mood of a space. Opt for candles, diffusers, or incense sticks that have soft, feminine scents like lavender, rose, or vanilla. These scents can calm your mind and make your living space feel more intimate and personal.

4. Feminine Finishing Touches

Consider the details that could femme up your space. How about some soft, flowing curtains that dance with every breeze? Or a vanity filled with all your makeup and beauty products, beautifully organized and displayed? Remember, it's these little touches that make your space uniquely yours.

5. Home Management Like a Princess

Managing a home is more than just keeping it clean. It involves scheduling, planning, and making sure everything runs smoothly. Create a daily, weekly, and monthly checklist of household tasks. Embrace tools and technology that can help you manage these tasks efficiently—perhaps a reminder app or a special planner dedicated to household management.

By the end of this subchapter, I hope you realize that decorating and managing your home is not just about aesthetics—it's about expressing and embracing your femininity. You're not just cleaning and organizing; you're curating a lifestyle that reflects your truest self. So, put on your cutest apron, and let's make your home as sissy-perfect as you are!

Remember, in every task you undertake, do it with love, sprinkle it with a bit of pink, and always, always keep it fabulously sissy!

Sewing and Craftsmanship

WELCOME TO A DELIGHTFUL section that is all about unlocking your creativity and finesse through the art of sewing and craftsmanship. If you've always admired the delicate details on dresses or wondered about stitching up cute accessories, then you're going to find this chapter both exciting and rewarding. Sewing isn't just a practical skill; it's a gateway to expressing your feminine side through colors, textures, and patterns that speak to your soul.

Why Sewing?

First, let's chat about why sewing is such a fantastic skill for anyone embracing their sissy persona. Sewing allows you to create unique garments and accessories that perfectly match your desired aesthetic. It's also a wonderful way to tune into a patient, focused state of mind. Imagine handling soft fabrics and crafting something beautiful from them – it's soothing and therapeutic!

Getting Started with Sewing

Starting with sewing can seem daunting, but let me guide you through this with some simple first steps:

1. Choose the Right Tools: Start with basic supplies like a sewing machine (a simple model will do), fabric scissors, pins, measuring tape, and threads of various colors. A small sewing kit can also be a handy addition.

2. Learn the Basics: Understand the basic sewing techniques like threading a needle, sewing a straight line, hemming, and stitching buttons. Plenty of online tutorials are available that are geared towards beginners. Don't rush; take your time to get comfortable with the basics.

3. Start Small: Begin with small, manageable projects. Perhaps a cute pillowcase or a simple tote bag? These projects are great for practice, and you'll feel a huge sense of accomplishment when you finish them.

Advanced Projects

Once you're confident with the basics, it's time to challenge yourself with more complex projects:

- Creating Your Outfits: Start with a simple skirt or a dress. Choose fabrics like cotton or satin that are forgiving and easier to work with. This can be your chance to experiment with different styles and patterns that enhance your sissy persona.

- Accessorizing: Sewing isn't just about clothes; it's also about creating accessories. Think about adding ribbons, beads, or lace to your creations to give them that personal touch.

- Custom Decor: Extend your sewing skills to create custom decor items for your home. Elegant curtains, plush cushion covers, or even a quilt can add so much personality and warmth to your living space.

Tips for Excellence in Sewing

- Patience is Key: Sewing requires patience, especially when you are just starting out. If you mess up, no worries! Unpicking a seam and starting over is totally normal.

- Practice Makes Perfect: Like any other skill, the more you sew, the better you will get. Dedicate time to practice regularly, even if it's just a few stitches every day.

- Join a Community: Look for local or online sewing groups where you can share your projects, get advice, and stay motivated. Community support is fantastic for learning and improvement.

Wrapping Up

Embrace sewing as a joyful journey into the world of fabrics, colors, and creation. Whether you're crafting a stunning dress or a simple scarf, each stitch you make is a step towards expressing your inner sissy princess. Remember, every thread woven is a reflection of your creativity and your transformation. Let's stitch up a storm and let your true colors shine through your creations!

Remember, developing your feminine skills through sewing and craftsmanship not only enhances your transformation but also adds a valuable and fun skill to your life. Happy stitching, and let the magic of the needle and thread lead the way!

Beauty and Self Care Rituals

HELLO, DARLING! WELCOME to the pampering world of 'Beauty and Self Care Rituals'. Whether you're already deep into your feminization journey or just starting to explore your sissy princess self, mastering the art of beauty and self-care is an essential step towards affirming your femininity.

1. Establishing a Skincare Routine

Every princess deserves glowing skin! Begin by understanding your skin type—oily, dry, combination, or sensitive—and tailor your skincare regimen accordingly. Start with the basics: a gentle cleanser, a moisturizer that suits your skin type, and sunscreen for protection against those harsh UV rays. Remember, consistency is key to unlocking the radiant skin of your dreams.

2. Hair Care is Self Care

Your hair is your crown, darling! Treat it with the love it deserves. Find a sulfate-free shampoo and a nourishing conditioner to keep your locks soft and healthy. Consider regular deep-conditioning treatments and don't shy away from experimenting with styles or colors that express your sissy self!

3. Makeup Magic

Makeup isn't just about beauty—it's about expressing who you are. Start with the basics: foundation matching your skin tone, a concealer for blemish-free skin, a splash of blush for a rosy glow, and mascara to open up those beautiful eyes. Experimenting with eye shadows and lip colors can be particularly thrilling. Remember, practice makes perfect and makeup should be fun, so enjoy your transformation with each brush stroke!

4. Nail the Look

Well-kept fingernails are a small detail that can say so much about your dedication to your feminization. Start with regular manicures—either at home or in a salon. Choose colors that reflect your mood or outfit, and don't be afraid to add some sparkle!

5. Scent Like a Princess

A lovely fragrance completes your transformation. Choose scents with floral or sweet notes which often evoke a feminine allure. Apply perfume on your pulse points—like your wrists, neck, and behind your ears—to leave a hint of enchantment lingering in the air wherever you go.

6. Diet and Exercise

Your outside is affected by what's inside. A balanced diet rich in fruits, vegetables, and lean proteins can improve skin, hair, and nails, and an effective exercise routine can help you maintain a soft, svelte figure. Find physical activities you enjoy, be it yoga, dancing, or cardio workouts, making sure everyone enhances your body in a way that feels affirming and joyful.

As you integrate these beauty and self-care rituals into your daily routine, remember that each step you take is a celebration of your ongoing transformation. This journey is yours and yours alone—be playful, be committed, and most importantly, be kind to yourself as you evolve into your sissy princess persona!

· · ⁓ · ·

IT'S ALL ABOUT LOVING who you are and expressing your femininity in ways that feel right to you. Each chapter of this eBook, especially this one on beauty and self-care, is crafted to help you embrace and express your sissy self with confidence and joy. So, keep practicing these rituals till they feel like second nature, and enjoy every moment of your beautiful transformation!

The Art of Seduction

HELLO, GORGEOUS! READY to dive into the captivating world of seduction? As a sissy in training, mastering the art of seduction is essential to your journey. It's not just about batting your eyelashes or wearing something provocative; it's an entire approach to ensuring you exude femininity and allure with every step you take. Let's explore how you can harness this power and transform into a sissy princess who can captivate any room!

Understand the Fundamentals of Feminine Appeal

Seduction begins with understanding the core elements that make femininity so enchanting. Embrace softness, gentleness, and the delicate art of flirtation. Your voice, your movements, and even your gaze can play pivotal roles in drawing others in. Practice speaking in a softer tone and experiment with the fluidity of your movements to add a touch of grace to your persona.

The Power of Eye Contact

Never underestimate the power of eye contact in the art of seduction. It can convey confidence, interest, and even a hint of mystery. When talking to someone, maintain steady, gentle eye contact. Let your eyes smile slightly, suggesting warmth. Remember, it's about creating a connection that feels both intriguing and inviting.

Dress to Impress

Your wardrobe is a key tool in your seductive arsenal. Choose outfits that accentuate your best features and reflect your sissy personality. Whether it's a flirty dress or cute, playful skirts, make sure each piece fits well and makes you feel fabulous. Use color and texture to your advantage - soft pastels, silky fabrics, and a bit of sparkle can go a long way in enhancing your seductive appeal.

Engage with Charm and Wit

Being seductive isn't only about looking the part; it's also about how you engage with others. Charm and wit can make you irresistible. Be genuinely interested in the conversation, listen actively, and sprinkle your dialogue with compliments that make the other person feel appreciated and special. Humor is a fantastic icebreaker, so a well-timed joke can lighten the mood and show off your playful side.

The Role of Body Language

Your body language speaks volumes. To project confidence and allure, practice good posture; hold your head high and your shoulders back. When seated, crossing your legs in a smooth motion can catch an eye. Subtle gestures, like a playful touch on the arm or tilting your head slightly during conversation, can intensify the personal connection you're aiming to build.

Continuous Learning and Practice

The art of seduction is an ongoing journey. With each interaction, you'll find new ways to refine your approach. Watch films, read books, and observe others who excel in their seductive abilities. Note what works and adapt those techniques to fit your unique style. Most importantly, practice regularly. The more you try, the more naturally it will come to you.

Embrace Your Inner Siren

Remember, at the heart of seduction is the ability to be completely in tune with yourself while being attuned to the desires of others. Embody the qualities you admire, and let them shine through in your interactions. By embracing the art of seduction, you're not just learning to captivate others; you're embracing a fundamental aspect of your sissy transformation.

Now, go forth and charm the world, you stunning sissy princess, you! And remember, every step you take in your heels is a step towards a more fabulous, seductive you. Let's make every moment count!

Chapter 8: Mental and Emotional Wellness

Building Confidence in Your Sissy Identity

Welcome to a pivotal section of your sissy transformation journey! Cultivating confidence in your sissy identity is not just about the external changes — it's also about nurturing your inner self. This part of the guide is designed to help you embrace and celebrate your sissy persona with confidence and pride. So, let's dive into some key strategies to build that unshakeable belief in who you are and who you aspire to be.

Understand Your Sissy Self

First and foremost, understanding the depths of your sissy identity is crucial. This means reflecting on what being a sissy means to you beyond the surface-level attributes. What emotions, behaviors, and fantasies do you associate with your sissy side? Journaling your thoughts can be a powerful tool here, allowing you to explore and affirm your feelings and experiences.

Surround Yourself with Positivity

Your environment can have a huge impact on your self-esteem. Strive to surround yourself with supportive friends, communities, and online forums that understand and celebrate the sissy lifestyle. Positive reinforcement from others who share or support your lifestyle can significantly boost your confidence and help you feel less isolated.

Celebrate Small Victories

Every step you take in your sissy transformation is an achievement. Celebrate these milestones, whether it's perfecting your makeup, mastering the sissy strut, or comfortably wearing your outfit in public. Acknowledging and celebrating these victories reinforces your identity and bolsters your confidence.

Visualize Success

Visualization is a powerful psychological tool. Regularly spend time picturing yourself as the confident, radiant sissy you aspire to be. Imagine interactions where you feel accepted and admired in your sissy role. Over time, these mental rehearsals can significantly impact your subconscious mind, boosting your real-world confidence.

Education and Reflection

Take time to educate yourself about the broader aspects of the sissy and broader LGBTQ+ communities. Understanding the historical and social contexts can enrich your sissy identity and provide a solid foundation of pride. Reflect on these learnings and how they relate to your personal journey.

Self-Care Practices

Confidence also comes from within, and taking care of your mental and emotional health is paramount. Engage in regular self-care practices that nourish both your body and mind. This could be through meditation, regular physical activity, or simply treating yourself to things that make you feel good.

Set Realistic Expectations

While being ambitious about your sissy journey is excellent, it's also important to set realistic goals. Unrealistic expectations can lead to disappointment and erode your confidence. Break your goals into manageable steps that you can realistically achieve and build upon.

Use Affirmations

Positive affirmations can reshape your thoughts and help you focus on your strengths. Use affirmations that reinforce your identity: "I am a beautiful, confident sissy," "I am proud of my femininity," or "I am worthy of respect and love." Repeat these daily to help cement a positive self-image.

By integrating these strategies into your daily life, you'll find that your confidence as a sissy will not just grow — it will flourish. This journey is about celebrating the unique, wonderful person you are, and every step forward is a step towards embracing your true self with confidence and joy.

Remember, your sissy identity is a beautiful aspect of who you are, and walking this path confidently opens up a world of fulfillment and happiness. Embrace it, celebrate it, and let your sissy light shine brightly!

Coping with Doubts and Society

HEY THERE, DARLING sissy princess! Let's talk about something really important today in your journey towards full feminization. We're navigating a path that might feel like a rollercoaster of emotions with ups and downs—some days you'll feel on top of the world, and others, not so much. This chapter is all about managing those tricky moments and dealing with societal opinions that might not always be favorable.

Understanding Your Doubts

First things first, it's perfectly normal to have doubts. Transformation isn't a straightforward process; it ebbs and flows. Think of your doubts as signposts, meant to make you pause and reflect. Ask yourself what's really behind these feelings. Often, you'll find it's fear of judgment or a misconception you've picked up along the way. Reflecting can strengthen your commitment and clarity about this fabulous journey you're on!

Self-Acceptance is Key

Before you can expect anyone else to accept you, darling, you've got to accept yourself. This includes embracing your desires to express yourself and your femininity in ways that feel right to you. Celebrate your bravery in taking steps to be the truest version of yourself. Remember, self-acceptance is a journey, not a one-time event. Be kind and patient with yourself.

Building a Supportive Community

You don't have to do this alone. There are many like-minded souls and supportive communities out there. Seek online forums, local groups, or even social media spaces dedicated to crossdressing or feminization. Connecting with others who are on similar paths can provide invaluable support and encouragement.

Dealing with Negative Society Reactions

Now, to tackle the elephant in the room—society. Unfortunately, not everyone will understand or support your journey. Prepare yourself mentally for potential negativity. A helpful tactic is developing a thick skin and focusing on the positive aspects of your transformation. Remember, the opinions that truly matter are those of people who support and love you.

Educate and Advocate

One of the strongest tools at your disposal is education. Often, negativity stems from ignorance. If you feel safe and comfortable, sharing knowledge about your journey can help break down stereotypes and encourage more open conversations. Additionally, becoming an advocate for your community not only helps you but also assists others who might be struggling with similar issues.

Seek Professional Help if Needed

There's absolutely no shame in seeking help from a mental health professional. It's important to maintain not just your physical appearance but also your mental and emotional wellbeing. Therapists who specialize in gender issues can offer you tailored advice and coping strategies, ensuring you remain healthy and happy through your transformation.

Stay True to Your Journey

Lastly, always remember why you started on this path. Hold onto the excitement and joy it brings you. Keep surrounding yourself with positivity, affirm your identity daily, engage in practices that bolster your mental health, and never hesitate to seek help when you need it.

Navigating societal pressures while managing doubts is a formidable task but remember, dearest, it's also a deeply rewarding one. Let your light shine bright, continue to grow your confidence, and let the world see the beautiful sissy princess that you are destined to become! Keep fluttering those lashes and strutting in those heels—because this is your path, and it's beautiful just like you.

Mindfulness and Meditation

HELLO, GORGEOUS! WELCOME to a serene corner of your transformation journey. In this chapter, we're diving deep into the tranquil waters of mindfulness and meditation, invaluable tools on your path to becoming a sissy princess. Remember, darling, this journey isn't just about the external changes; it's also about embracing your inner beauty and peace. Let's get started!

Why Mindfulness?

In the whirlwind of our everyday lives, especially during such a profound transformation, it's easy to feel lost or overwhelmed. Mindfulness is your anchor; it grounds you. By becoming more aware of the present moment, you can enjoy experiences, understand emotions, and learn more about yourself. This is particularly powerful as you navigate through your feminization training.

Meditation—Your Secret Garden

Think of meditation as your private retreat. Here, you can shed any stress or negativity, and just be. Meditation promotes emotional health, reduces stress, and improves concentration. For someone embracing their sissy self, these benefits can fortify your commitment and enhance your journey's joy.

How to Begin

- Find Your Space: Start by choosing a quiet, comfortable spot where you won't be disturbed. It could be a cozy corner of your room with cushions or a snug spot by your window.

- Set the Scene: Consider dim lighting or candles and perhaps a diffuser with some calming lavender oil.

- Ease Into it: Begin with just a few minutes a day. Sit comfortably, close your eyes, and focus on your breath. Inhale peace, exhale tension.

- Guided Meditations: Sometimes, guidance helps. There are plenty of apps and videos out there designed to guide you through meditation practices. They can be particularly useful when you're starting out.

Daily Practice

Try incorporating short mindfulness exercises throughout your day. Take a moment to really savor your morning tea or coffee, or spend a few minutes breathing deeply before starting your makeup routine. These little pauses can significantly increase your mental clarity and emotional stability.

Emotions Are Your Friends

During your feminization training, you'll experience a spectrum of emotions. Mindfulness helps you understand and respect these feelings, not as obstacles, but as steps towards deeper self-awareness and acceptance. When you feel joy, sink into it; when it's something less pleasant, explore it without judgment.

Long-Term Benefits

As you make these practices a regular part of your life, you'll notice changes. Your stress levels might drop, your overall happiness might increase, and you'll likely find your training becoming more enjoyable and profound. Plus, these skills are transferable to every part of your life, enhancing relationships and personal resilience.

Connect With Others

Why not bring mindfulness into your social interactions? When meeting with friends or engaging with your community, be fully present. Listen intently and speak authentically; you'll find your connections deepen, enriching your journey even more.

Sweetheart, remember, mindfulness and meditation are not just practices but ways of living. They beautify your internal landscape just as much as your external transformation does. By embracing these practices, you cultivate not only a sissy princess's poise and elegance but also a beacon of calm and positivity in your world.

Now, take a deep breath, darling. You're doing wonderfully, and this chapter is just another step in your fabulous journey. Keep shining!

Understanding and Expressing Your Emotions

•• ❧ ••

HEY THERE, LOVELY! As we embark on this exciting journey of transformation together, it's not just about the physical aspects of becoming a sissy. Equally important—if not more—is your mental and emotional wellness. This part of the guide is dedicated to helping you explore and express your emotions authentically and freely. So, let's dive in, shall we?

Emotions: The Heart of the Transformation

Understanding and managing your emotions is pivotal in your transformation journey. Remember, becoming a sissy is not just about dressing up or acting in a certain way; it's about really connecting with your feminine side emotionally and mentally.

1. Identifying Your Feelings

Start by recognizing your emotions. Are you feeling happy, sad, anxious, or excited? Sometimes, these can be complex and mixed, but that's okay. Acknowledging them is the first step towards understanding them.

2. Expressing Your Emotions

As a sissy, expressing your feelings can be very freeing. Whether it's through writing, talking with friends, or even practicing facial expressions in the mirror, find a way that feels right for you. This expression is your strength, not a weakness.

3. Emotion-Driven Decision Making

Being in touch with your emotions can actually help in making decisions that are more aligned with your true self. This alignment is crucial as you continue with your feminization training.

4. Dealing with Negative Emotions

It's inevitable to encounter negative emotions. When this happens, try to understand the source of these feelings. Is it fear of judgment, insecurity, or something else? Addressing the root cause can help you manage them more effectively.

5. Cultivating Positive Emotions

Surround yourself with positivity. Engage in activities that make you feel good, listen to uplifting music, or watch inspiring movies. Positive emotions can boost your morale and keep you motivated throughout your transformation.

6. Emotional Resilience

Building emotional resilience is key. This means not just handling the ups and downs more smoothly but also emerging stronger from each challenge. Remember, every step forward in this journey makes you more resilient.

Enhancing Your Emotional Vocabulary

Sometimes, the challenge is not just feeling emotions but expressing them accurately. Enhance your emotional vocabulary by learning new words that describe different shades of emotions. This practice will not only help you in understanding your own feelings better but also in communicating them more effectively to others.

Support Systems Are Crucial

Never underestimate the power of a good support system. Friends, family, or a community of fellow sissies can provide emotional support, understanding, and encouragement. Sharing your feelings with them can lighten your emotional load and provide different perspectives.

• • ❧ • •

NOW, READY FOR THE next step? Keep flipping through our eBook for more insightful guides and tips. Together, we'll make sure your journey is not just about looking the part but feeling it deeply and authentically. Let's make this transformation as fulfilling and joyous as possible!

Remember, every step you take on this path is a building block to becoming not just a sissy but a happier, more fulfilled you. So, cherish and embrace your emotional experiences—they are what truly enrich your journey.

Seeking Support and Community

EMBARKING ON YOUR FEMINIZATION journey can be an exhilarating yet challenging experience. In this chapter of "Sissy School: A Comprehensive Guide to Feminization Training," we delve into an essential aspect of your transformation: finding emotional and mental support. Engaging with a supportive community not only enhances your journey but also helps to foster growth, acceptance, and confidence.

Finding Your Tribe

The journey towards becoming a sissy princess may sometimes feel isolating, but remember, you're not alone! Connecting with others who share your passion and experiences is not just comforting—it's empowering. Look for online forums, social media groups, or local meet-ups that focus on feminization and the broader context of gender expression. Platforms like Reddit, FetLife, and specialized forums provide safe spaces to ask questions, share experiences, and connect with individuals on similar paths.

Embracing Virtual Support

In today's digital age, support is often just a click away. Engage in webinars, follow influencers in the feminization community, and consider joining virtual support groups. These resources can be invaluable for sharing tips, emotional support, and gaining diverse perspectives on the feminization process. Virtual connections can also pave the way for friendships that transition into the real world.

The Importance of Meetups and Events

Whenever possible, participate in local events or gatherings. These can range from support groups to themed parties, workshops, and conferences centered on LGBTQ+ themes, particularly focusing on cross-dressing and feminization. These events not only allow you to learn from experiences shared by peers and experts but also help you in normalizing and celebrating your identity.

Support from Professionals

Sometimes, the guidance you need might be more specialized. Consider seeking support from therapists or counselors who specialize in gender issues. Professionals can provide tailored advice and strategies to cope with any emotional or psychological challenges you may encounter. Moreover, they can help in reinforcing positive self-image and dealing with societal pressures.

Building a Personal Support System

Besides finding community support, it's crucial to cultivate a personal network which may include friends, family, or partners who respect and support your journey. Open communication about your needs and experiences can foster deeper relationships and a supportive personal environment.

The Power of Mentorship

Finding a mentor who has successfully navigated this path can be a turning point in your journey. A mentor can offer practical advice, emotional support, and insights from their own experiences. The relationship can also challenge you to grow and embrace your new identity more fully.

．．⤸．．

REMEMBER, SEEKING SUPPORT and creating a community is not a sign of weakness, but a strategy for resilience and success.

Through community, we find strength. Each person's journey is unique, but you don't have to walk it alone. As you progress through your transformation into a sissy princess, let community be your unwavering support.

By fostering connections and seeking out those who understand and uplift you, your path through feminization will be enriched with joy, camaraderie, and a deeper sense of self-acceptance.

Chapter 9: Lifestyle Integration

Living Full-Time as a Sissy

Hello, darling! You've made some incredible strides on your journey, haven't you? Stepping out in full sissy attire for special occasions or private parties is thrilling, but have you ever fantasized about embracing your sissy identity full-time? Well, buckle up because we're diving deep into what it means to live day-to-day as a sissy princess!

Embrace Your New Normal

The first step toward living full-time as a sissy is embracing this as your new normal. This is about more than just the clothes or makeup; it's about accepting and affirming your identity in every aspect of daily life. Begin by gradually incorporating more feminine items into your everyday wardrobe. Soft, delicate fabrics or subtly cute accessories like a charm bracelet can affirm your sissy identity even in mundane settings.

Create a Sustainable Routine

Consistency is key. Develop a daily routine that includes time for your dressing, skincare, and makeup. Remember, feminization is not just an external transformation but an internal one too. Include practices that help you maintain a feminine posture and voice modulation. It might feel overwhelming at first, but with time, these will become second nature.

Social Transitions

As you begin to live as a sissy full-time, there will be social transitions too. It's important to prepare for different reactions from people in your life. Start with a supportive community — perhaps friends from the feminization circles or online groups — who understand and respect your lifestyle.

Workplace Adaptation

Navigating professional life might be challenging. Check your workplace policies on dress codes and conduct. In some cases, you might need to have open conversations with your HR department or supervisors. The goal is to integrate smoothly while being true to your sissy identity.

Handling Public Interactions

Going out in public can be daunting. Confidence is your best accessory here. Walk with your head held high and interact with grace. People may stare, but remember, most are just curious. Your comfort and safety are paramount, so always trust your instincts about when and where it's safe to express yourself openly.

Self-Care and Mental Health

Living full-time as a sissy can be emotionally taxing. Regular self-care routines can help manage stress and maintain mental health. Consider therapy or support groups experienced with gender identity issues to provide that extra layer of emotional support.

Celebrate Your Journey

Every day you live authentically is a victory. Celebrate your milestones, big or small. Perhaps keep a diary or blog about your experiences. Sharing your story not only affirms your life but also inspires others who might be considering a similar path.

Living as a sissy full-time is certainly not without its challenges, but it's also filled with moments of joy and self-discovery. It's a deeply personal decision and one that requires courage and resilience. But remember, darling, you're not alone. Within the pages of this book and beyond, a community of support and love awaits to lift you up.

By tackling each element thoughtfully and lovingly, integrating your sissy persona into your everyday life will not only be possible but profoundly rewarding. Keep fluttering those lashes, swaying those hips, and never forget—each step in those lovely heels is a step towards the truest version of you. Welcome to your fabulous sissy lifestyle, princess!

Balancing Professional Life

HEY THERE, GORGEOUS! As you embark on this fabulous journey of feminization and embrace your sissy persona, one of the trickiest terrains to navigate might just be your professional life. It's all about finding that perfect balance where your sissy identity and career harmoniously coexist. Let's dive in and explore some practical ways to merge these aspects of your life while keeping it fun and empowering!

1. Assess Your Workplace Environment:

First things first, understanding the environment of your workplace is key. Not all offices are created equal—some may be more conservative, while others might celebrate diversity and self-expression. Gauge how open your workplace is to personal expression and consider how much of your sissy identity feels safe to share.

2. Subtle Transformations:

If you're in a more conservative environment, think about subtle ways to express your sissy self. This could be as simple as adding some flair to your outfit with accessories or choosing pastels or floral patterns for your ties or socks. Every little element counts and helps you stay connected with your sissy side.

3. Time Management:

Balancing a professional life and your personal transformations requires astute time management. Allocate specific times for your dressing and sissy activities that do not interfere with your work commitments. Remember, a stress-free sissy is a happy sissy!

4. Digital Persona:

In the digital age, your online persona can also reflect your sissy identity. Use your personal social media platforms to express this side of you, but always be mindful of privacy settings and potential overlaps with professional colleagues.

5. Networking:

Connect with other sissies who might be facing similar challenges. Online forums and local support groups can provide valuable advice and a supportive community that understands exactly what you're going through.

6. Personal and Professional Growth:

Use your journey as a sissy to fuel your personal and professional growth. The confidence and self-understanding you gain can lead to better performance at work and a more fulfilled life. Embrace your unique perspective and let it shine in your professional interactions.

7. Handling Challenges:

Challenges are inevitable, but how you handle them defines your experience. If faced with adversity, seek to educate and advocate calmly. Remember, your goal is to build bridges, not walls. Professional counselling or speaking with HR can also be steps you can take if you feel conflicted or misunderstood.

Navigating your professional life as a sissy doesn't have to be a daunting task. With the right strategies and a sprinkle of sissy sparkle, you can excel in your career while being true to your fabulous self. Keep shining, keep thriving, and remember—all parts of your life deserve to be celebrated!

With these tips, not only will you manage to keep your sissy identity vibrant, but you'll also ensure that your professional life flourishes. Remember, integration is key, and with a bit of planning and a lot of self-love, you'll master the art of balance. So go ahead, strut into your office with confidence, ready to tackle whatever comes your way with a bit of extra sissy flair!

Sissy in Social Settings

HELLO, DEAR READER! ◈ Ready to take your sissy transformation out into the wider world? Venturing into social settings might seem daunting, but it's a fabulous way to express your new identity and grow your confidence. Let's make your journey as smooth and enjoyable as possible with these useful tips and thoughtful insights.

Start Small and Stay Comfortable

Initially, choose low-pressure social situations to test the waters. It could be a supportive friend's house party or a gathering with others from the sissy community. Start where acceptance is expected to boost your confidence.

Dress Appropriately

One of the keys to feeling great and fitting in is dressing appropriately for the occasion. Aim for outfits that are not just pretty but also suitable for the setting. A cute, modest dress might be perfect for a casual meetup, while something a bit more glamorous could be saved for a special night out.

Develop Your Social Skills

As a sissy, expressing yourself with both your appearance and your manners is important. Practice polite conversation, learn to listen actively, and always be mindful of the nuances of interactions. Compliments can go a long way—offer them sincerely and often!

Safety First

Always prioritize your safety. Be mindful of the environments you're entering and the people you're meeting. If you're going out to new places, consider having a trusted friend accompany you. Also, stay informed about your local area's attitude toward the LGBTQ+ community.

Handling Negative Reactions

Despite the progress made towards acceptance and equality, not all spaces are equally welcoming. If you encounter negativity, stay composed and remove yourself from the situation if possible. Surround yourself with supportive people who make you feel appreciated and loved.

Connect with the Community

There's strength in numbers! Connecting with the sissy community or broader LGBTQ+ groups can provide you with support and advice tailored to your experiences. It's also a great way to make friends who understand what you're going through.

Reflect and Grow

After social outings, take some time to reflect on your experiences. What did you enjoy? What would you like to improve? Viewing these experiences as learning opportunities can significantly enhance your confidence and skills in social settings.

Remember, integrating the sissy lifestyle is a journey, not a race. Take it one step at a time, and most importantly, enjoy the process. Each social interaction is a building block to becoming the unabashed, proud sissy princess you aspire to be! 😊◈

By following these tips, you'll not only manage social settings with greater ease but also find genuine joy in expressing your sissy identity. Embrace each moment with confidence and charm—your unforgettable presence is your truest power in any room!

Legal Considerations

HEY THERE, LOVELY SISSIES! As you dive deeper into the sparkling world of feminization, it's super important to chat about some of the legalities you'll want to keep in mind. Entering this glittery lifestyle is all about expression and joy, but let's make sure you're doing it safely and within the framework of the law. So, let's organize our frills and get down to business with some key legalities. ◈

Understanding Legal Boundaries

First things first, embracing your sissy self and expressing it shouldn't be cause for legal worries, right? Absolutely! However, laws can vary wildly depending on where you live, so it's vital to know your local regulations regarding dress codes, identity expression, and public behavior. Some regions are super chill and accepting, while others might be more conservative.

◈ *Tip: A quick check with local LGBTQ+ organizations can give you a wealth of info on your area's stance and any advocacy or legal support you might find helpful.*

Privacy Matters

Privacy is a biggie. Whether you're attending sissy school classes, shopping for your outfits, or participating in events, think about how public or private each space is. Online, be cautious with what personal information you share. Protecting your identity starts with knowing who's trustworthy.

◈ *Remember: Just because a website or group says it's for sissies, doesn't mean they have your best interests at heart. Do your research!*

Employment and Discrimination

Now, let's talk about the real world. Jobs, careers, and workplaces — how does being a sissy fit in there? In many places, employers are becoming more open to diverse expressions of gender identity, thanks, in part, to enhanced anti-discrimination laws. But there's still a way to go.

◈ Action Step: Understand your rights at work. If you're unsure, legal counsel or speaking to an HR professional about gender expression rights might help.

Navigating Public Spaces

Whether you're out on the town or just doing everyday things, knowing how to navigate public spaces while fabulously expressing your sissy self can sometimes be tricky. Always prioritize your safety. If you ever feel unsafe, having a buddy system or knowing safe spots can make all the difference.

⚖ Legal Insight: Check if your area has any specific laws about attire in public spaces. All set? Go forth confidently!

Consent is Key

This is a golden rule: always, always ensure that all parties are consenting, especially when you're interacting more intimately or exploring new boundaries within the sissy lifestyle. Consent should be informed, enthusiastic, and ongoing. This guards your well-being and ensures all interactions are respected and legal.

◈ *Sissy Wisdom: Communication is your crown jewel. Clear, open talks about expectations and boundaries keep everyone in the know and happy.*

By keeping these legal considerations in mind, you can focus more on flourishing as a sissy princess and less on unnecessary hurdles. Remember, knowledge is power — especially when paired with a fabulous pair of heels and the right dash of attitude! So strut your stuff, keep informed, and embrace your transformation with both excitement and a smart awareness of the world around you. ◈

Long-Term Goals and Planning

HELLO, MY DAZZLING sissy princesses! As you step delicately into the enchanting world of feminization, it's crucial to focus not just on the frills and laces but also on sculpting your journey with clear, long-term goals and detailed planning. Here's a friendly guide to help you seamlessly integrate your sissy persona into your everyday lifestyle, ensuring a transformation that is both fulfilling and fun.

Set Clear Feminization Goals

Start by envisioning where you want to see your sissy self in the future. Are you looking to embrace femininity at special events only, or are you planning a full-time transition? Setting specific, measurable, and realistic goals will keep your journey on track. For instance, aim to master the art of makeup or walking in high heels by a particular date. This way, you can celebrate small victories that will motivate you further on your sissy path.

Draft a Feminization Roadmap

A well-laid plan is your best friend! Break down your goals into smaller, manageable tasks. If your aim is to develop a feminine voice, start with voice training exercises, gradually increase your practice sessions, and perhaps, consult a voice coach. Creating a step-by-step roadmap will not only make the process less daunting but also more systematic.

Education and Learning

The journey of becoming a sissy princess is as much about learning as it is about transforming. Immerse yourself in books, videos, and other resources that delve into feminization techniques, lifestyle tips, and the psychological aspects of gender identity. Knowledge is power, and the more you know, the more confidently you can navigate your transformation.

Community and Support

No princess should feel alone in her castle! The sissy community is vibrant and supportive. Engage with community forums, attend events, or join online groups where you can share experiences, seek advice, and make friends who understand and encourage your transformation journey. Remember, every sissy's journey is unique, and sharing your story can be incredibly empowering for yourself and others.

Regular Reflection and Adaptation

As you progress in your sissy training, take time to reflect on your experiences. What's working? What isn't? Perhaps certain aspects of your feminization are more challenging than anticipated. Regular reflection allows you to adapt your goals and methods, ensuring they align with your evolving sissy identity.

Personal Safety and Comfort

While embracing your sissy persona, personal safety and comfort should always come first. Always navigate your transformation at your own pace and within environments where you feel safe and accepted. Setting boundaries is not only okay, it's necessary to ensure that your journey is positive and healthy.

Celebrate Every Milestone

Every step you take in your sissy transformation is an achievement. Celebrate your milestones, no matter how small they may seem. Whether it's perfecting your sissy strut or receiving compliments on your appearance, celebrating these moments can significantly boost your confidence and reaffirm your commitment to your sissy journey.

Embarking on this fabulous road of feminization with clarity and well-structured planning will set you up for success. Remember, the journey is as wonderful as the destination, and every little step is a sparkle in your tiara. Embrace it, enjoy it, and let your sissy flag fly high!

Chapter 10: Advanced Feminization Assignments

Public Outings and Experience Building

Hello fabulous readers! Welcome to one of the most thrilling sections of your feminization journey: Public Outings and Experience Building. Whether you're just dabbling in dressing up or you've been indulging in your sissy personality in the privacy of your home, taking it to the streets can be exhilarating yet intimidating. Fear not, for this guide is designed to help you confidently step out and embrace your sissy persona in the public eye.

Stepping out into the world in full sissy regalia is a bold move, and it requires courage, planning, and a pinch of audacity. But I assure you, the rewards are worth every bit of effort. Public experiences not only enhance your comfort and confidence but also deepen your understanding and acceptance of your sissy identity. Let's dive into how you can make these outings both successful and enjoyable.

1. Start Small: It's okay to feel a bit nervous at first. Begin with less crowded places, perhaps a friendly neighborhood or a quiet time of the day. This will help you adjust slowly without feeling overwhelmed.

2. Safety First: Always consider your safety when planning an outing. Choose environments that are known to be inclusive and sissy-friendly. Inform someone you trust about your plans whenever possible.

3. Dress Appropriately: While you might love your most extravagant outfits, consider the context and location for your outings.

Sometimes blending in a bit can help make your experience more comfortable and less stressful.

4. Behavioral Tips: Observing and mimicking the gestures, walk, and mannerisms typically ascribed to females can add a lot to your experience. This not only helps in blending in but also in feeling the part more authentically.

5. Embrace the Experience: Allow yourself to enjoy every moment. Whether it's shopping, walking in a park, or having a coffee, immerse yourself in the experience. Interact with people, make conversations, and remember, confidence is your best accessory.

6. Reflect and Learn: After each outing, take some time to reflect on what went well and what could be improved. Did you feel comfortable? How did people react? Was there something that made you feel particularly happy or uneasy? Use these reflections to plan better next time.

7. Join a Community: There are many online forums and local communities for sissies and cross-dressers. Being a part of such groups can provide you with support, advice, and more importantly, companionship on your public outings.

Public outings are a monumental step in your feminization process. They validate your identity and expressions in real-world scenarios, pushing the boundaries of your comfort zone towards a more inclusive society. Remember, every big change starts with a single, small step. So, put on those heels, wear that fabulous outfit, and step out with your head held high. Remember, sissy, you are born to shine!

Through gradual exposure and these practical tips, your public outings will go from nerve-wracking to exhilarating in no time. Each outing is a unique adventure and a step forward in your journey of self-discovery and acceptance. Embrace the challenges and celebrate your milestones as you transform into the sissy princess you aspire to be. Get ready to sashay your way through the world with poise, grace, and a sparkle that's all your own!

Advanced Makeup and Styling

HELLO GORGEOUS! WELCOME to the exciting world of advanced makeup and styling, where you'll learn how to transform into the ultimate sissy princess. Whether you're heading out for a night on the town or just fancy a glamorous day at home, mastering the art of makeup and styling is essential to enhancing your feminization journey. So, let's dive into some fabulous techniques and assignments designed to elevate your skills to a professional level!

1. Mastering the Art of Contouring and Highlighting

Contouring and highlighting can dramatically alter the appearance of your face, accentuating your feminine features. Start by selecting a contour shade slightly darker than your skin tone and a highlighter that is lighter. Carefully contour your jawline, cheekbones, and the sides of your nose. Highlight your cheekbones, brow bones, cupid's bow, and the bridge of your nose. This will help create a more defined, feminine facial structure.

2. Eye Makeup Extravaganza

Eyes are the windows to the soul, and in sissy makeup, they're your chance to really sparkle! Learn to use bold eyeshadows, venture into the world of glitter, and perfect your eyeliner wing. Experiment with colors that complement your eye color and skin tone. Don't forget volumizing mascara or, for that extra glamorous look, false eyelashes that can give your eyes that captivating, dramatic flair.

3. Flawless Foundation Routine

A smooth, flawless foundation is key to a polished look. Choose a foundation that matches your skin tone and apply it evenly to achieve a seamless finish. Use a damp beauty sponge for application to avoid a cakey appearance and set your foundation with a light dusting of translucent powder to ensure it stays in place all day.

4. Lipstick and Lipliner - Perfect Your Pout

No sissy transformation is complete without a stunning lip. Start with a lip liner to define the shape of your lips, making them appear fuller and more pronounced. Choose bold lipstick colors such as pinks, reds, or even purples to make a statement. Remember, the key is precision, so take your time to apply and consider using a lip brush for a more professional finish.

5. Hairstyling Hacks

Your hair is your crown and deserves just as much attention as your makeup. Explore feminine hairstyles that frame your face and fit your personality - whether it's soft curls, bold bobs, or long, luxurious waves. Learn to use hair accessories effectively, such as bows or floral pins, which can add a touch of elegance and charm to your overall look.

6. Pulling It All Together - Outfit Selection

The final step in your styling is the outfit. This should mirror the effort and theme of your makeup and hair. Opt for clothes that flatter your figure and express your sissy persona. Whether it's cute dresses, skirts, or blouses, choose outfits that make you feel confident and beautiful.

Each of these steps serves as an assignment. Practice them regularly to refine your skills and express your feminized self with confidence and style. Remember, the goal is not just to look like a sissy princess - but to feel like one, too! Embrace each step, experiment with different styles, and most importantly, have fun with your transformation journey. Keep shining, you fabulous sissy princess, you!

Perfecting the Art of Flirting

HELLO, LOVELY! IN THIS chapter, we dive deep into what it means to not just understand, but master the captivating art of flirting as a sissy princess. Whether you're aiming to charm a room full of admirers or entice that special someone, the flair of flirting is an essential skill in your feminization journey.

Why Learn to Flirt?

Flirting is more than just batting your eyelashes or offering a coy smile; it's about communicating attraction and interest through both verbal cues and body language. For a sissy princess, learning this art can enhance your ability to express your femininity and connect with others on a more intimate level.

Body Language Basics

Start with the way you carry yourself. Feminine movements tend to be softer and more fluid. Practice moving with grace and poise. When you flirt, use gentle gestures like a touch on the arm or leaning in slightly – these signal interest and engagement. Mirroring the body language of the person you're flirting with can also create a sense of connection and rapport.

The Power of Eye Contact

Eyes are the windows to the soul, and maintaining eye contact is key to showing confidence and interest. However, there's a flirtatious twist to it for a sissy princess – a lowered gaze followed by a playful look up through your lashes can be incredibly alluring.

What to Say and How to Say It

Flirting involves playful, engaging conversation that can make your counterpart feel special and desired. Compliments are your best friend here. Be specific in your praise; instead of generic compliments, focus on what uniquely attracts you to the person. Phrasing your words with a bit of shyness or hesitation can also add to your feminine allure.

Listening is Seductive

Being a good listener is crucial. Pay close attention to what the person says, and respond thoughtfully. Showing genuine interest in someone's thoughts and feelings can be more appealing than any outfit or makeup.

Practice, Practice, Practice!

Like any other skill, the art of flirting requires practice. Engage in social situations, experiment with different styles of flirting, and observe what works best for you. Remember, confidence grows with experience.

Keep It Fun and Respectful

Flirting should always be enjoyable and consensual. It's important to read social cues and ensure that your attention is welcomed. Respect boundaries, and never be afraid to step back if the interest isn't mutual.

Wrapping It Up

Perfection might be a high bar, but improvement is always within reach. With each step forward, you not only enhance your flirting skills but also embrace and express your feminized persona more confidently. So go ahead, my dazzling sissy princess, flirt your heart out and let your charming self shine through!

Flirting isn't just about making someone else feel good; it's about embracing your femininity and enjoying the moment. Keep this guide handy and refer back whenever you need a little boost. With practice and confidence, you'll find that perfecting the art of flirting will not only be enjoyable but will also enrich your journey in becoming the ultimate sissy princess. Happy flirting!

· · ⌒ · ·

Etiquette Classes and Workshops

WELCOME TO ONE OF THE most transformative sections of our journey – Etiquette Classes and Workshops! If you are dreaming of becoming the quintessential sissy princess, mastering the subtleties of etiquette is a must. In this chapter, I'll guide you through the nuances of feminine poise, grace, and manners that are essential in your sissy transformation.

Understanding Etiquette Importance

First things first, why is etiquette so crucial? Etiquette is the set of conventional rules governing social behavior in any society. For a sissy, mastering this is not just about knowing which fork to use at dinner (although that's also important!). It's about embodying the grace and courtesy expected of a lady. It influences how you are perceived and, significantly, how you feel about yourself. Proper etiquette sets the foundation for your interactions, ensuring you appear polished and respectful.

Core Elements of Feminine Etiquette

Feminine etiquette can be quite broad, but let's focus on the essentials:

- **Posture and Poise:** A sissy must exude elegance through their posture. Always stand straight, shoulders back, with a slight, natural curve in the lower back. When seated, legs should be gently together or crossed at the ankles, never the knees.

- **Polite Conversations:** Communication is key. Always listen attentively, and when you speak, keep your tone gentle and your words considerate. Avoid interrupting others, and remember to use 'please' and 'thank you'.

- **Dining Debonaire:** From navigating a formal table setting to eating gracefully, dining etiquette is pivotal. Practice using utensils the right way and take small bites. Remember, no elbows on the table!

Workshops to Consider

Joining workshops can be highly beneficial. These classes provide not only theoretical knowledge but also practical, hands-on experiences which are invaluable. Here are a few types of workshops to consider:

- General Social Etiquette: Covers basic social etiquette rules, including polite conversation and being a gracious guest or host.

- Dining Etiquette Workshops: Focuses on table manners, use of silverware, and dining conversation.

- Posture and Poise Classes: Often offered by dance studios or finishing schools, these classes help you embody grace in your movement.

Practice Makes Perfect

Like any other skill, perfecting your etiquette requires practice. Incorporate these practices into your daily routine to make them second nature. Remember, the goal is not to feel constrained by rules but empowered by them. Embracing these practices enhances your feminization journey, making you not just look but also feel like a sissy princess.

• • ⚮ • •

THIS FASCINATING WORLD of feminine grace awaits you. Dive in, practice diligently, and watch as your sissy transformation becomes complete, embodying the charm and poise of a true princess. Happy learning!

Undergoing Professional Training

HELLO THERE, GORGEOUS! It looks like you're ready to step up your game in the sissy princess transformation journey. This part of our guide is all about taking your feminization to the next level with professional training. Wondering why you might consider this step? Let's dive in!

Why Professional Training?

While self-training is fantastic, there's something uniquely effective about professional help. Professionals can offer you personalized insights and corrections that are hard to spot by yourself. They come with a wealth of experience in helping individuals just like you blossom into their sissy persona.

Finding the Right Trainer

The perfect trainer should be someone well-versed in feminization training, respectful, and supportive of your goals. This could be a dominatrix specialized in sissy training, a lifestyle coach, or even a voice feminization instructor, depending on what aspects you feel you need the most help with.

What to Expect from Professional Sessions

Sessions can vary widely, but here are a few common elements:

- Personal Assessment: An evaluation of where you stand and what your specific needs are.

- Targeted Exercises: Be it walking in heels, mastering makeup, or perfecting your feminine voice, each session will likely focus intensely on specific skills.

- Emotional Support: A good trainer also provides emotional and psychological support, which is invaluable.

The Benefits

- Accelerated Learning: With focused help, you can learn more quickly and efficiently.

- Custom Tailored Advice: Get advice and tips tailored specifically to you.

- Confidence Building: Professionals not only teach skills, they also help build your confidence in your new identity.

Making the Most of It

1. Be Open: Share your fears, desires, and challenges. Transparency can greatly enhance the quality of your training.

2. Practice: Whatever you learn, practice it. Repetition is key to mastering any new skill.

3. Feedback: Ask for feedback constantly. It helps you improve and the trainer understand your pace and style of learning.

Professional training can be a significant investment in both time and money, but the personalized attention and expertise can elevate your transformation journey hugely. It's like having a fairy godmother who's equipped with all the right magic to help you shine!

As you consider stepping into professional training, remember that every step forward is a step towards realizing your true self. Embrace the learning curve, enjoy the process, and let your beautiful sissy self-flourish. We believe in you, so march forward with all the grace and boldness of a true sissy princess!

Keep shimmering!

Chapter 11: Erotic Practices and Safety

Understanding Sissy Fantasies and Desires

Hello, aspiring sissy princesses! Navigating through the intricate world of sissy fantasies and desires is both exciting and essential for your journey in feminization. In this section, we'll dive deep into the psychological tapestry that forms the basis of sissy fantasies and unpack how you can safely explore these tantalizing desires.

Exploring the Landscape of Sissy Fantasies

Sissy fantasies can range from the desire to wear feminine clothing to engaging in role plays that affirm your sissy identity. It's important to recognize that these fantasies are a form of self-expression and are as diverse as the individuals who harbor them. By understanding your unique desires, you can tailor your feminization training to best suit your transformation goals.

Identifying Your Sissy Desires

Start by asking yourself what aspects of feminization draw you in. Is it the allure of lingerie, the demeanor and poise of femininity, or perhaps the dynamic of power exchange? Writing these down can help you pinpoint your interests and set clear paths for your training regimen. Remember, understanding is the first step to a fulfilling sissy lifestyle.

Safety First: Navigating Your Fantasies Responsibly

While indulging in your sissy fantasies, keeping safety as a paramount concern is crucial. Always engage in activities that feel comfortable and stop any encounter or practice that feels harmful or unsettling. Consent and communication with involved partners are the cornerstones of a safe and enjoyable experience.

Practical Steps to Safe Exploration

1. Educate Yourself: Knowledge is power. Read, learn, and converse about various aspects of the sissy lifestyle to better understand its dynamics and nuances.

2. Establish Boundaries: Knowing your limits and communicating them clearly to any partners involved is critical. Use safe words and discuss limits before engaging in any scenario.

3. Gradual Progression: Start slowly with your fantasies. If you're new to feminization, begin with less intensive practices and gradually build up as you become more comfortable and confident.

4. Self-Reflect: Periodically reflect on your experiences. What did you enjoy? What didn't work for you? This reflection will guide your ongoing sissy journey and help refine your desires and limits.

Concluding Thoughts

Understanding and embracing your sissy fantasies is a thrilling part of your transformation. By approaching these desires with an informed and cautious mindset, you ensure a journey that is not only safe but also deeply satisfying. Remember, being a sissy princess is all about finding joy and authenticity in your feminization practice. So lace up your corsets, adjust your tiara, and step forward confidently into the enchanting realm of your sissy desires. Let this guide be your trusted companion as you explore the depths of your fantasies with care and passion!

Safe and Consensual Practices

HEY THERE, LOVELY SISSY-in-training! As you blossom into your sissy princess self, it's crucial to prioritize not just the frills and thrills but also safety and consent in your journey. This section of our guide is dedicated to ensuring your exploration is as safe as it is thrilling.

Understanding Consent

Consent is the golden rule in any interaction but especially critical in the BDSM and feminization scenes. It's not just about saying yes or no; it's about understanding and agreeing to specific activities beforehand and having the freedom to express when something isn't right for you. Always ensure that all parties involved are fully informed, agreeable, and comfortable before starting any activity. Remember, consent is continuous and can be withdrawn at any time, so keep communication open and ongoing.

Creating a Safe Word

A safe word is a must in your playful explorations. This is a pre-agreed word or signal that will immediately stop any activity whenever uttered. Choose something unusual that wouldn't naturally come up in regular conversation. Consistency is key—once the safe word is used, all activity stops, no questions asked. This is a non-negotiable trust pact between you and your play partners.

Knowing Your Limits

It's okay to push boundaries, but knowing and respecting your limits and those of your partners is crucial. Start slowly, especially if you are new to any practice. Discuss boundaries with partners clearly before engaging in any scene. Over time, you may adjust these limits, but never feel pressured to engage in activities that make you uncomfortable.

Safety Gear and Tools

Depending on the activities you explore, certain gear and tools might be necessary. For instance, if bondage is an element of your play, invest in high-quality restraints that won't break and can be easily removed in case of emergency. Always educate yourself on the proper use of any new tools or toys, and prioritize quality over cost to ensure safety.

Aftercare is Essential

Post-scene, physical and emotional aftercare is essential. Whether it's cuddling, debriefing the experience, or treating any physical discomfort, aftercare helps both you and your partners transition back to everyday life and processes the experience. This nurtures trust and care in your dynamic and is a fundamental part of any responsible practice.

Remember, lovely, the aim is to have fun and explore your sissy persona in a safe, consensual environment. Each assignment and practice should bring joy and tap deeper into your desired sissy princess identity. So lace up, practice safety, and let the glam begin responsibly!

By honoring these guidelines, you ensure that your journey into feminization is not only exhilarating but also respectful and secure, paving the way for many more delightful experiences in your transformation.

Exploring BDSM and Kink in Feminization

WELCOME TO ONE OF THE most thrilling parts of your feminization journey—exploring the realms of BDSM and kink! As we dive into this topic, it's vital to approach with an open mind and an eagerness to learn about the dynamics and practices that can enrich your transformation into a sissy princess.

Why BDSM and Kink?

BDSM (Bondage, Discipline, Sadism, and Masochism) and other kink practices offer a playground for exploring power dynamics, pleasure, and the psychological depth of your sissy persona. These experiences can intensify your feminization process by connecting deeply with your submissive side, enhancing your sensations, and pushing the boundaries of your conventional sexual expression.

Setting the Scene

Before you start, it's crucial to understand the fundamentals of BDSM which are built on the pillars of trust, consent, and negotiation. Discuss boundaries, desires, and safe words with your partner. This ensures that every act performed is consensual and enjoyable for both parties.

Gear and Attire

Investing in the right attire and gear can significantly impact your experience. Consider items that accentuate your feminized form—corsets, high heels, stockings, and lingerie that not only look good but make you feel completely immersed in your sissy role. For BDSM activities, you might want to explore cuffs, ropes, gags, and blindfolds, always ensuring they are safe and suitable for beginners.

Roles and Dynamics

Feminization within BDSM can involve different roles such as sissies, maids, or baby dolls, each bringing unique elements to the play. You might be a submissive sissy serving your dominant partner, or perhaps a naughty schoolgirl in a playful scenario. Understanding these roles and finding what resonates with you and your partner can enhance your connection and enrich your experience.

Safe Practices

While exploring these new horizons, always prioritize safety. Be aware of both physical and emotional limits, and keep communication open with your partner. It's important to continually educate yourself about the tools and practices you're engaging in. Remember, a good scene is one where all parties feel respected, cared for, and fulfilled.

Aftercare

After exploring intense scenarios, aftercare becomes a cornerstone of BDSM. This may involve cuddling, debriefing about the session, or simply spending quiet time together. Aftercare helps in grounding both partners, addressing any emotional or physical impacts, and strengthening the relationship.

Ready to Explore?

As you begin this exciting aspect of your feminization training, remember that patience and continuous learning are your best tools. Start slowly, gauge your comfort levels, and gradually expand your boundaries. Your exploration of BDSM and kink is a personal journey that should be fun, safe, and empowering.

So, slip into your favorite sissy attire, set your boundaries, and let your exploration lead you into thrilling new territories of self-expression and pleasure. Happy exploring!

Privacy and Security in the Sissy Lifestyle

HEY THERE, LOVELY! As you embark on your journey to become a dazzling sissy princess, it's crucial to keep a sparkling tiara on safety and privacy. Navigating this path can be thrilling, but ensuring your well-being is paramount. So let's dive into some essential tips that will keep you secure while you explore and enjoy your new lifestyle.

Understand Your Boundaries: First and foremost, know your limits and clearly define them. It's okay to say no, and it's important to communicate what you're comfortable with to your partners or community. Your boundaries are valid, so respect them and ensure others do too.

Privacy is Key: In the digital age, keeping your sissy activities discreet might be sensible, especially if you're not ready to share this part of your life with everyone. Use pseudonyms or aliases online, be cautious about what information you share, and consider using privacy-focused communication tools for chats or meetings.

Secure Your Environment: Whether you're dressing up at home or attending a sissy event, make sure your environment is safe. If you're meeting someone new, vet them as much as possible, arrange meetings in public spaces initially, and always inform a trusted friend about your whereabouts.

Health and Safety Comes First: Engage in safe practices, especially when exploring the more erotic aspects of being a sissy. This means regular health checks, using protection, and being mindful of both physical and emotional health. Don't shy away from consulting healthcare providers who are open and supportive of the LGBTQ+ community.

Embrace a Support Network: Having a tight-knit, trustworthy group can significantly enhance your security. This community can offer advice, share experiences, and provide emotional support. Plus, it's always more fun to have fellow sissy friends on your fabulous journey!

Legal Awareness: Be aware of your rights and the laws in your area regarding expression, behavior, and anti-discrimination protections. It helps to know what legal support is available to you, should you ever need it.

Security in the sissy lifestyle isn't just about locking doors; it's about ensuring emotional, physical, and digital safety in a world that might not fully understand or accept you yet. By setting clear boundaries, ensuring privacy, and engaging safely and healthily in your activities, you can shine bright like the sissy princess you are destined to be.

Keep twirling that skirt with confidence, knowing you're smart about your security!

Health and Hygiene

HELLO, LOVELY! AS YOU embark on your journey to becoming a fabulous sissy princess, there's one golden rule you must always keep in mind: Health and Hygiene are paramount. Let's dive into why keeping squeaky clean and healthy not only ensures your well-being but also enhances your transformation experience.

1. Skincare and Beauty Regime:

Looking flawless isn't just about the makeup—it starts with a great skincare routine. As a sissy, it's essential to develop a personalized skincare regimen that keeps your skin glowing and smooth. Begin with the basics: cleansing, toning, and moisturizing daily. Always remove your makeup before bed to avoid clogged pores and breakouts. Consider visiting a dermatologist or a beauty specialist who can advise you on products suitable for your skin type.

2. Hair Care Matters:

Whether you rock wigs or style your own hair, proper care is crucial. For wig lovers, ensure you wash and condition them periodically, using products specifically designed for wig care. For natural hair, a gentle shampoo followed by a hydrating conditioner will keep your locks luscious and ready for any style.

3. Feminine Hygiene:

Maintaining good feminine hygiene practices is vital, especially when you're involved in erotic sissy activities. Regular baths or showers, using unscented soaps to avoid irritation, and keeping your body areas dry to prevent infection, are all essential steps. If you're exploring deeper feminization, such as tucking, make sure you're doing it safely and hygienically to avoid any health risks.

4. Regular Health Check-ups:

Regular visits to your healthcare provider are non-negotiable. These check-ups aren't just for maintaining general health; they're also an opportunity to discuss any modifications in your feminization process. Be it hormonal treatments or other related procedures, professional medical advice is crucial.

5. Safe Sex Practices:

As a sissy engaging in erotic play, practicing safe sex is a must. Use protection during all sexual encounters to prevent STDs and other infections. Be informed about your partners' health status, and don't hesitate to discuss health checks candidly. Remember, it's your right and responsibility to ensure the safety of both yourself and your partners.

6. Nutrition and Exercise:

A balanced diet and regular exercise regime will keep you in shape and support your feminization goals. Focus on foods rich in antioxidants and nutrients. Also, incorporate exercises that enhance the body areas you wish to feminize—like squats for a more voluptuous rear or pelvic floor exercises for core tightening.

Keeping these elements in check will not only assist you in looking your best but feeling great too! Remember, being a sissy is not just about the external transformation; it's about taking care of your internal health and hygiene as well. So, pamper yourself, stay clean, and keep shining, you beautiful sissy princess!

Stay fabulous and always keep safety sexy!

Chapter 12: Celebrating Your Sissy Transformation

Documenting Your Journey

Hello, gorgeous! You've embarked on such a remarkable transformation journey, becoming the sissy princess you always dreamed of being. As you progress, it's essential to keep a record of your fascinating transformation—not only to see how far you've come but to share your story and inspire others. Here are some tips on how you can effectively document your journey.

Start a Journal

Journaling is a fantastic way to track your experiences and emotions throughout your sissy training. You might start by writing a few sentences each day or even detailed entries when you feel inspired. Include your triumphs, setbacks, and everything in between. Over time, those little entries will weave into a comprehensive narrative of your transformation.

Take Photos and Videos

Visual documentation is super powerful! Periodic selfies and videos in your favorite outfits or practicing your sissy mannerisms can be so rewarding. Seeing the visual evidence of your transformation can be empowering and is a wonderful tool to reflect on your progress.

Create a Blog or Vlog

Why not share your journey with the world? Starting a blog or a vlog can not only document your experiences but also connect you with a community of like-minded individuals. Share tips, celebrate milestones, and discuss the challenges you've faced. It's a great way to get support and affirmations from others who are on similar paths.

Set Milestones and Celebrate Achievements

Establish clear milestones in your journey, such as mastering a new voice pitch or perfecting your walk. Each achievement is a stepping stone in your journey and deserves celebration. Documenting these moments can serve as motivation for you and for others who follow your journey.

Reflect on Your Progress

Every month, take some time to reflect on your documentation. Look through your journal, photos, video clips, or blog posts to see how much you've changed. This reflection is not only about appreciating your outer transformation but also about recognizing the inner growth that you've achieved.

Your journey is unique and incredibly personal, but sharing it can be both liberating and inspiring. Documenting this process helps solidify your identity as a sissy princess and can become a beacon of hope and encouragement for others walking the same path. So, keep shining and showing off that fabulous progress!

By keeping these tips in mind, you'll make sure that every aspect of your sissy transformation is celebrated and remembered. Can't wait to see how you sparkle, darling!

Creating a Sissy Milestone Calendar

EMBARKING ON YOUR SISSY transformation journey is thrilling, and like any significant venture, it benefits from both structure and celebration. One delightful way to keep your spirits high and your goals in sight is by creating a Sissy Milestone Calendar. This fun and practical tool serves as a roadmap and a cheerleader for your evolving sissy identity.

Why Create a Milestone Calendar?

Transformation journeys, particularly those related to personal identity and lifestyle changes, are marathons, not sprints. It's easy to lose sight of how far you've come, which can result in feeling discouraged or stagnant. A milestone calendar helps you visualize your progress, celebrate your successes, and stay motivated through each phase of your transformation.

Getting Started: What to Include

1. Important Dates: Mark the start of your journey, anticipated key milestones, and a projected 'graduation' or completion date. Remember, these dates aren't set in stone but serve as motivational markers.

2. Assignments and Tasks: From your book "Sissy School: A Comprehensive Guide to Feminization Training", pick over 100 assignments that you find most compelling. Schedule these assignments throughout your calendar, balancing easier tasks with more challenging ones to keep your journey engaging.

3. Reward Points: Set up a reward system for each milestone you achieve. Whether it's treating yourself to a new outfit, a night out, or something else you cherish, acknowledging your hard work is crucial.

4. Reflective Days: Schedule days to reflect on your journey. Reflective days are essential for appreciating the depth of your transformation, making adjustments to your trajectory, and setting new goals if old ones no longer suit you.

Crafting Your Calendar

Digital or physical? While a digital calendar (using tools like Google Calendar or Trello) offers reminders and mobility, a physical calendar can be crafted to reflect your personality. Decorate with stickers, colorful markers, or anything that resonates with your sissy persona.

Using Your Calendar

- **Daily Check-In:** Spend a few minutes each day with your calendar. This routine can help keep your goals front and center.

- **Adjust as Necessary:** If a scheduled milestone no longer feels appropriate, adjust it. Your transformation is unique, and so should your calendar be.

- **Celebrate Publicly or Privately:** Some might enjoy sharing their progress with a close friend or online community, while others might prefer a private celebration. Do what feels best for you.

A Sissy Milestone Calendar isn't just a schedule; it's a narrative of your personal journey, a scrapbook of your transformation, and a testament to your determination. Creating and maintaining one can significantly enrich your experience, providing structure, motivation, and a whole lot of fun along the way.

As you fill out each milestone, you'll not only be closer to becoming the sissy princess you aspire to be, but you'll also have a vivid record of your journey, a storyline that's uniquely yours. Let this calendar be your guide, your motivator, and your celebratory confidante. So grab your stickers and your pen—your fabulous sissy transformation awaits, one sparkle-filled milestone at a time!

Throwing a Sissy Coming Out Party

CONGRATULATIONS ON reaching this wonderful milestone in your journey! Your sissy transformation is a remarkable achievement that deserves celebration. Hosting a 'Sissy Coming Out Party' can be the perfect occasion to showcase your newfound identity, revel in your achievements, and affirm your place within the community. Here's how you can throw a fabulous party that'll be the talk of the town!

1. Pick a Theme:

Every great party starts with a fantastic theme! Consider themes that resonate with your personal style and transformation journey. From a 'Pink Princess Gala' to a 'Retro Diva Disco,' the theme should reflect elements of your sissy persona that you're most proud of. Decorate accordingly to set the mood and create an immersive experience for your guests.

2. Invitations:

Create eye-catching invitations that give your guests a hint of what's to come. Whether it's lacy patterns, glittery accents, or soft pastels, make sure your invitations scream fabulousness. Be clear about the party details and consider adding a dress code to match your theme.

3. Venue:

Choosing the right venue is crucial. It might be your own home, which can be a comfortable and controlled environment, or perhaps a rented space if you're expecting a larger crowd. Ensure the venue matches your party size, aesthetic, and offers enough privacy for you and your guests to enjoy freely.

4. Entertainment:

A sissy coming out party isn't complete without some engaging entertainment. Think about hiring a DJ for a dance party or perhaps a local drag performer who can add flair and excitement. Include games and activities aligned with your theme—like a makeover station or a fashion runway where guests can show off their own transformations.

5. Dress to Impress:

Your outfit on this day should be a showstopper! Choose an ensemble that makes you feel confident, gorgeous, and true to your sissy identity. Whether it's a sparkling gown, a cute maid outfit, or something uniquely your style, wear it with pride.

6. Capture the Moments:

Make sure to hire a photographer or set up a photo booth with lots of fun props. These photos will be cherished keepsakes commemorating your journey and celebration.

7. Favors:

Send your guests home with something memorable. Party favors could include personalized items like keychains, cookies in the shape of high heels, or even thank-you notes expressing your appreciation for their support and love.

8. Speech or Thank You Note:

Prepare a little speech or a heartfelt thank you note to acknowledge those who've supported you throughout. This can be an emotional highlight, reinforcing the personal significance of your journey and the celebration.

Your 'Sissy Coming Out Party' is not just a party; it's a proclamation and a chance to bask in the joy of your true self. Enjoy every moment, surround yourself with love, and let your sissy flag fly high. You've worked hard to get to this point—now it's time to celebrate all things sissy with flair and extravagance!

Sharing Your Story

CONGRATULATIONS ON reaching this chapter, darling! You've ventured on an incredible journey of self-discovery and transformation, evolving beautifully into your sissy princess persona. Now, it's time to step into the light and share your unique story.

Why Share Your Story?

Sharing your journey is not just about recounting tales; it's a powerful tool for self-affirmation and for inspiring others. By articulating your experiences, you validate every step and challenge you've overcome, reinforcing your identity and perhaps, most importantly, showing others they're not alone in their own journeys.

How to Share?

1. Personal Blogs:

Start a blog to chronicle your journey. This is a private, yet public enough space where you can express your thoughts and feelings openly. You can interact with readers, receive feedback, and connect with a community that relates to your experiences.

2. Social Media Platforms:

Platforms like Instagram or TikTok are perfect for visual and dynamic expressions of your new self. Share photos, short videos, and stories about your transformation milestones. Remember, a picture is worth a thousand words!

3. Support Groups:

Join support groups for sissies and gender exploration communities. These are safe spaces where individuals share stories, struggles, and successes. Hearing about other experiences similar to yours can be incredibly validating and emotionally enriching.

Crafting Your Story

Be Honest and Open:

Your authenticity is your strength. Share both your triumphs and your setbacks. It makes your story relatable and real.

Highlight Key Moments:

What were the turning points in your journey? Reflect on those significant episodes that had profound impacts on your transformation – like the first time you dressed up or how you felt meeting others like you.

Share Practical Tips:

What helped you most? Was it a specific book, a friendship, or a particular mindset? Give practical suggestions that can help guide others who are at the beginning of their transformation journey.

Keeping It Positive

Remember, the primary goal of sharing your story is to inspire and enlighten. Keep your narrative positive and hopeful. Show the joy and fulfillment that embracing your sissy self has brought to your life.

Respect Privacy

While sharing, always keep in mind the privacy of others involved. Obtain consent if your story includes anyone else. And, if you prefer, you can always share anonymously or under a pseudonym.

• • ❧ • •

BY SHARING YOUR STORY, you not only carve out your identity but also amplify the voices of countless others in the sissy community. You contribute to a greater narrative of acceptance and diversity, acting as a beacon for those still finding their way.

Darling, you are an inspiration. Your journey, now told in your words, will light up paths and encourage hearts. Shine bright, sissy princess!

Continuing Education and Evolution

CONGRATULATIONS ON reaching this joyous phase of your journey! By now, you've embraced incredible changes and celebrated many milestones in your sissy transformation. However, this is just the beginning of a beautiful, ongoing adventure in feminization. Let's talk about how you can continually evolve and keep the excitement alive in your sissy lifestyle!

Never Stop Learning: The world of feminization is vast and varied. There are always new skills to master, trends to follow, and personal limits to push. Consider diving deeper into specific aspects like makeup artistry, fashion styling, or even voice feminization techniques. Online courses, tutorials, and workshops can be excellent resources. Engaging regularly with content that enriches your understanding and skills will keep your journey fresh and exciting.

Build a Supportive Community: Surround yourself with like-minded sissies and allies who celebrate and support your lifestyle. Online forums, social media groups, and local meet-ups can be fantastic places to connect with others on similar paths. Sharing experiences, tips, and challenges not only helps you grow but also reinforces your sense of belonging in the sissy community.

Reflect and Set New Goals: As you achieve the goals you initially set, it's important to reflect on your progress and set new objectives. Maybe you've mastered walking gracefully in heels, and now you want to learn how to dance in them. Setting progressive goals keeps your transformation exciting and ensures that your journey remains fulfilling.

Stay Updated: Fashion and femininity are ever-evolving, mirroring changes in society and culture. Keeping yourself updated with the latest in women's apparel, makeup innovations, and cultural shifts in gender expression will help you stay relevant and varied in your transformation. Subscribe to newsletters, follow influencers in the feminization sphere, and participate in community discussions to stay informed.

Self-Care is Key: Amidst all the excitement, don't forget to take care of your mental and physical well-being. Engaging in regular wellness activities, like mindfulness, yoga, or even pampering yourself with spa days, can greatly enhance your overall experience. After all, a happy and healthy sissy is a beautiful sissy!

Celebrate Regularly: Finally, make it a point to celebrate your achievements, no matter how small they might seem. Each step forward in your sissy transformation is a victory worth celebrating. Arrange little celebrations for yourself; perhaps treating yourself to a new outfit, a fancy dinner, or a night out with friends. These celebrations not only boost your morale but also affirm your identity and progress.

By embracing continual education and evolution, you ensure that your journey as a sissy remains as thrilling and fulfilling as the day you started. Remember, every step forward is a step toward becoming the ultimate sissy princess you aspire to be. Keep shining, keep learning, and most importantly, keep celebrating every moment of your fabulous transformation!

Don't miss out!

Visit the website below and you can sign up to receive emails whenever Mistress LaLa publishes a new book. There's no charge and no obligation.

https://books2read.com/r/B-A-POZKB-TRSHD

BOOKS 2 READ

Connecting independent readers to independent writers.

Also by Mistress LaLa

Sissy School: A Comprehensive Guide to Feminization Training

Milton Keynes UK
Ingram Content Group UK Ltd.
UKHW020824141124
451205UK00012B/711

9 798223 577034